Life in the Aftermath of a Psychopath

… An Evaluation of my Personal Experience in the Era of President Donald Trump

Becky Joyce Reed

DEDICATION

A tremendous note of appreciation to this gift of awareness – at times terrifically painful , but ultimately breathtaking in being able to view the participants of life with hi-definition clarity.

Reality will wage heavy combat to maintain the old order.

CONTENTS

Memory

ACKNOWLEDGMENTS

A huge thank you to Sandra L. Brown (*Women Who love Psychopaths,How to Spot a Dangerous Man*) and her site (saferelationshipsmagazine.com), Thomas Sheridan (*Puzzling People: the Labyrinth of the Psychopath*), Robert Hare as a foremost expert on psychopathy (*Without Conscience: the Disturbing World of the Psychopaths Among Us*), *Malignant Self Love: Narcissism Revisited*, by Sam Vaknin, and one of my initial introductions to the awareness, Dr. M. Scott *Peck's People of the Lie.* In addition, Betty La Luna's expansive blog collections under "Narc Raider," therapist Robert O'Connor, and therapist Peter Shepherd (www.trans4mind.com). These are amazing sources to begin one's understanding.

"To Let Go of Pain, The Idea of Changed Belief is Sitting on the Sidelines Waiting." ~Me

1
THE BACKDROP

My tale of myself before an encounter with an out-of-sync being and the transmogrify through this slipping-of-reality experience shows me as a funny, upbeat gal trudging through the mire of devastating quicksand and finally coming out the other side. The loss of Faith entailed more than a flattening of my belief systems, but also the forming of my emotions, enthusiasm, and hopes and dreams into a bland clone of their former presences.

In the war-torn land with a psychopath, **Life** reigned in Chaos.

Make no mistake, you have been at war.

This is my personal mirror of hindsight...and promise of wondrous tomorrow. You will find yourself – after the anguish, disbelief, and sense of abandonment – a better version of you! The process is a tough one.

I am not attempting to clinically differentiate between the terms of narcissist and psychopath. The world of narcissism/psychopathy left me exhausted and terrified - there was no empathy for me as a being. I was only a tool to be used. In my mind I picture myself as a water skier being yanked behind a high speed motorboat within the grasp of a stormy sea...and I refused to let go of the rope.

All the emotions that popped on stage with pretense of sincere caring and connectedness were simply character devices. I had been so bombarded with a perpetual stream of demands, lack of sleep, gas lighting, tests to prove my worth as a wife and for the clan, and almost round-the-clock inundation into their belief systems of using others and the general assemblage of living, I suffered a type of relationship Stockholm Syndrome. When my utilization purposes ended, I was cut from the clan as coldly and precisely as if it were a surgical procedure. I was no longer valuable to these people. It was a long journey back to find myself.

The strange morals of the group always left me feeling out-of-focus. There are many of us survivors and we are taking steps to reclaim our lives. I knew Cinderella would still have to clean the castle and that the Prince would be away on exciting travels. I had sought the fairy tale and although aware, knowledgeable, and eager for a new adventure, found myself lost in a panic-filled fun house of terror.

Life in the Aftermath of a Narcissist, my first book, came into being as I worked to create my life again following the utter anguish of being used and manipulated by the husband I cherished and who, I believed, loved me. In the midst of heartache and disbelief, I found myself to be dealing with the memories of gas lighting, my devastated emotions, a financial outlook of sheer decimation, and the loss of just "who I was."

Marrying on the heels of my completion of *Romance Stew*, a cute dittie, I was, at age 55, heady at finding "Mr. Right." The man and his family filled my heart's empty spaces with hopeful expectation in discovering love with all the trimmings and a caring extended family. However, with a narcissist it felt like I had enrolled in a master's degree program on ever shifting sands of reality.

I had participated in acquiring practical knowledge in the arena of romance and relationships and I was "seasoned" at that age, recognizing that *Love* doesn't always bring the curtain down on a happily-ever-after theme. Even so, I sought enough good times to offer balance with life's rough patches. Meeting "my particular" narcissist proved such a disconcerting trek into unknown territory. Loving and losing as I have described in my journey's discourse was to be a learning experience beyond any I could have fashioned in my wildest fantasies. This jaunt through the bowels of "the Twilight Zone" found me feeling as if I had joined a traveling circus from an alien planet.

To attempt to have the reader comprehend this horror story and not feel it's all oh-so dramatic from a "victim's" capacity, I would urge everyone who comes to these books to find the film, "The Night Listener." It was written by Amistead Maupin and stars Robin Williams. The tale is an excursion into horror for anyone of ethical standards. Williams' character is a night radio show host who is given a moving manuscript written by a young boy who was horrifically abused. His social worker now had custody of him.

As Williams' character is drawn deeper into the emotional entanglement with these two, he begins to question their actual identities and even his own reality in the way he connects with them. He is a man of genuinely high levels of warmth, love, and deep empathy. Unfortunately, the entire production of the relationship has been only a fabricated charade. The sensation is one of being "out-of-space and time," leaving the host to sort his compassion, awareness of intellect, and his own desire to believe in an idea where he wanted to be of benefit. He now must also handle this feeling of excruciating vulnerability. In the convoluted association much of his life has unraveled as his time, energy, and ability to realign focus to his own personal life and goals has disintegrated. This movie brought back the anguish of my own "episode of *The Twilight Zone*" within a fairy tale.

The relentless surprises from the onset of my marriage, following a whirlwind courtship, proved extremely costly. It seems that my substantial funds vanished into the black hole of financial crises brought by my spouse and his family almost in the blink of an eye as I struggled to maintain the marriage. His IRS debt from the past raised its ugly head. The arrival to live with us of the "bipolar," alcoholic adult son with expensive legal problems set the stage for chaos and highlighted my lack of savvy in standing my ground in this alien domain, away from my family and friends.

Along with this came the drunken, drugged out former sister-in-law who called incessantly, leaving explicit boy-toy messages for my spouse. I always felt such an affront all the more so because my husband really had no desire for intimacy with me, but acquaintances whom I deemed knowledgeable urged me not to overreact. I was immediately saddled with all the household expenses and even the cell phones for his son and parents....and of course, the never totally "in the past" first wife. My mother-in-law had held her close to "the family core" through the decades since their divorce and my spouse's former re-marriage.

My invalid mother-in-law living within a half hour drive felt me to be a coupon from heaven as I planned to use my money to add to the household coffer while I worked on writing. She called 4-6 times a day and there was forever some need of chauffeuring, errand, transportation, housework requirement, help to her husband, or trip to a doctor or therapy required. I felt that I had chosen this man whom I loved and, therefore, also his family and discerned that the marriage vows required persistence to that commitment.

Now I can say with a chuckle as I look back that *I was the only participant in agreement with this thread of belief*. Soon his online contacts, re-connections with women of the past, and virtual dating began. Following the "I Do's," I was informed that my spouse was bipolar and I required that we meet his therapist. The tie between these two was immensely close and she supplied him with excuses for his behaviors, all the while telling me how important it was that I carry such a load in the family setting.

A bank levy followed with a lengthy unpaid period of illness soon after. Finally, the light glimmered weakly at the end of the tunnel...until, seeking marriage counseling, I suggested that his mother might be perpetrating emotional incest with her desires for me to call him her pet names, have her name be placed on all my gifts to him, and wanting details of any sexual intimacy. I became quickly disavowed, unceremoniously discarded. *Apparently auditions for my replacement had been underway and the next lady chosen.* **Not only "left for dead," there would be no closure.**

With the passage of year five climbing from the quicksand in this strange adventure within the aftermath, I still struggle with the financial debacle and emotional triggers, but hope exists.

I suspect I've taken down my "romance at all costs" shingle from my front doorway. But, I'll look in on it and shine it from time to time. I did seek that elusive "Camelot" of high adventure with its invention of fanciful sentiment. Although I did encounter and even initiate heroically marvelous deeds in the quest for my evasive dream, the lighthearted zest more than occasionally found itself dashed by life's details and unexpectedness.

So, now, with a limited arsenal of skills, I can share my story with you. In the process, I have connected with the most amazing people, mostly women, who have taken the same path. Their passages shared for the aid of others along the route fill me with awe, humility, and joy at the depth of humanity and compassion.

You can SURVIVE.
I have....
The next goal...
TO THRIVE.

"No matter what people tell you, words and ideas can change the world." ~ from "Dead Poets Society"

2
NOW AT AGE 63

As anguish filled as the experience with my ex-spouse, a psychopath, was, it left me rejuvenated in ways I never would have believed to be beneficial. When all the hormones were flowing and youth still paid a visit, I felt it acceptable to do a headstand to wriggle into my jeans. In a way, that is exactly what I had done with this individual finding his home somewhere on the continuum of narcissism to psychopathy.

I still disagree with the idea that co-dependence is the explanation for me (and SO many), but I do now feel that the vibrations of essence that I exuded, pulled that specimen into my life sphere. Websites seem to be popping up all over in which this experience surfaces. The take on life's path that I accepted played out dramatically with my heartbreak in finding myself dispossessed from my position in my well-heeled reality.

Pretty darned theatrical in hindsight, but at that time I surely felt betrayal. Most especially the sense of perfidy about life and my own evaluations of it. Maybe there was some arrogance on my part that I would be above such treachery. I will even allow scope for the idea that I deceived myself to some degree while keeping while keeping in mind that my moral compass was pointed in the right direction.

Now, almost a decade outside the fray, I can honestly say that it is true that I am not the same. When I would espouse that during the beginning stages of self-recovery I felt a terrific loss of something that I deemed valuable about myself. I did so with such a weight of the taste of harm and injustice.   This juncture in time finds me different....and from a point of power in self-awareness. Who in the world would have imagined I could arrive at this post of calm-without-pain?   In my case the travel through menopause simultaneously developed. There is something to be said for the absence of those jolly, blindfolded and rampaging hormones.

**I can agree with George Carlin:
"Some people see things that are and ask, Why? Some people dream of things that never were and ask, Why not? Some people have to go to work and don't have time for all that."**

And this is perhaps the wisdom of a kind of coming-of-age and the willingness to grasp the "as is" of living. Even with the plethora of answers and reasoned analyses for what appeared a wasteland under the umbrella world of a psychopath, one simply puts one foot forward each day... in the aftermath.

In an episode of *The Mary Tyler Moore Show,* Mary's character is bemoaning the fact that her life is dull and humdrum. In a monotone voice she says, "I get up, have breakfast, go to work, come home, eat, go to bed, and start again." Ted Baxter, her narcissistic co-worker and perhaps a few bricks shy of a full load, tells her in one of his amazingly few moments of bright awareness: "Just change it to (now in high-energy and upbeat voice) I wake up, have breakfast, go to work, come home, to to bed, and start all over again."

Ah....just a bit of truth in a nutshell.

I have come to the realization that my experience brought me back to a dexterity of perception of New Age-y thought patterns...in a good way. Still, one has to really LOOK at what is happening and recognize the players. Once-upon-a-time I felt there was good in everyone and with my fixed moment in the "bowels of the Twilight Zone," I came to see *evil* in the lack of empathy, remorse, and any ability to comprehend the life force of another.

My evaluation now is that these presences are totally unfamiliar, strangely frightening, and something that I do not wish to have in my sphere of living. It is fool-hardy to expect a wolf in the wild not to attack a flock of sheep when ravenous. Our power comes from realizing that we have the choice to see how one opens himself and that there is no longer a need to do so. **Choose your people...there do exist vampires among us.**

I do find that I am more ready to take a stand when my beliefs come under siege. However, there is a void of that passion to go out of my way to live beyond the quiet life I have preferentially selected. *With much humor I will share that the absence of stimulating hormones plays a large part of the staging to my needs today.*

There are times in my newly appreciated zone where I do not desire to acquiesce to make others more comfortable. My background of money-making resume slots includes self-employment with a cleaning service, stint in law enforcement, lab tech, writer/researcher for a web page, care attendant, property manager, and now, night janitor which permits me time flexibility to care for and love unconditionally my grandchildren. With no short supply of rather caustic humorous temperament at times, I occasionally wish for fewer Ph.D's and more folks with unadorned common sense.

To this end I have severed some connections in my realm: a cousin who forever held herself as being interminably *right,* judgmental and never meeting an unkind thought she failed to voice; those whose New Age themes suggested a *sit back and let the universe handle everything* motif of style; and my own need to "communicate" when such was not required or even desirable.

I will proffer some of my less than pristine reactive behaviors in the aftermath of my internment with "crazy town." Once past the stage of utter and excruciating pain colored by that life of imprisonment, I found a new platform of anger. Not about those involved in denigrating and working me as a hired hand, but much like a Don Quixote of sorts...often tilting at windmills...sometimes without the advertence of the victims. I realized I had to beware my blasé approach because other people were affected. I found that deep within a bubbling fury could hit blast off, well past full throttle. It's tough to diagnose myself as a "nobody in a somebody world.

In my accountability awareness, I have not always been pleased that my resultant behavior caused stress and upset. Entitlement blatantly exhibited could throw my dark imagination into overdrive, wishing a dreadful fate upon these folks. I could almost feel a rising tide of willingness to strike out without reason or thought of consequences in chasing the scent of blood in the air. I could envision them gutted between the front bumper of an 18-wheeler and the asphalt. I was rather calm, cool, and collected before my encounter with **my** psychopath and his taker-clan. This is not the route of behavior I would have chosen before my marriage to the users and belittling clique. But, this is part of the corollary backwash. The journey in the aftermath is not only of evaluation, but of resetting one's personal ethics.

The consequential time after living with a psychopath for several years left me with more than emotional outbursts and some character flaws, and included real measurable physical and health issues – not to mention property damages with which to deal after giving my ex his "head," and physical issues of dysfunction and pain. The harm to my sense of self-worth continued as I fought to survive with being left-for-dead financially – for putting food on the table, money to pay rudimentary bills of survival, and the need for transportation. I had allowed myself to be worked as slave labor and the knee surgery did not evolve as predicted. I came away with damage and a body worn out from physical demands as well as stress depletion. I located a personal care provider who worked with me on time frames/physical therapy suggestions/and medications that would permit me to handle the pain during shifts in employment. My knees and lower legs took a beating when a table and tires fell on me...not to mention the lifting of the dead-weight wheelchair bound mother and completing the ex's stockade fencing. The problem in this aftermath is to recognize that these *things were not done* to *me in a vacuum.* I gave my consent and this is the part that needs to be viewed.

It appeared that my escape from the insane asylum had not been a clean one. I felt a bit like Jon Ronson in seeing these presences everywhere. In an oddly facetious way, I was in the same boat as Erma Bombeck's character a mother who misunderstands the use of the playpen and climbs into it herself.

My obligatory demand for moving along life's path in the quiet, unassuming lane had me working alone as a night housekeeper for a school. In this slot I was privy to the trickle down dramatic interactions between all the members of the teaching staff, administrators, and kitchen help. It can be painful to watch as those of the "in" group harp on missteps by any on the outside...and the resultant self-chastising to those wounded. I remember being in love with my work in the past, but I have noted that it isn't just within me, but others as well that find themselves without this emotional bond. For me, the skill set that I possess of time prioritizing and organization finds a home in the lower order but non-repetitive work using awareness, overview of the larger picture, and freedom of leeway...I only press my two-cents' worth when I comprehend the negative play. Sometimes the workforce hostilities border on the illegal. Our world seems to have changed. Whether hidden before or simply not highlighted, there exist clashes with the haves-vs.-have-nots. Injustice flows under particular hierarchical dominions of power. I had previously genuinely believed that working hard and being reliable was ll that one needed to succeed well.

Nonetheless, as Vernon Howard says, "blundering progress is still progress." As the wake of my ordeal with a psychopath and his taker-clan loses energy the farther the motorboat moves ahead. I can feel that life once again belongs to me...and is good. It can still be a tough go at times.

I suspect my rekindling of my relationship to God/Universal Energies has to do with my moving out of a 2-D existence which served as a gray-shaded prison. Faith, to me, means a re-connection to the grand choice for decency, betterment, joy, and making a difference. Faith is like a family member who holds your hand through joys and upsets. The rules come not from dogma but from a most personal "feel" for rightness.

"I do believe at the end of the night when you're with your family, the character gets hung up on the door like a coat, and is there to be taken on the next morning" ~ Liam Neeson

3
THE CARHARTT

Gianni Versace is right. "Don't be into trends. Don't make fashion own you, but you decide what you are, what you want to express by the way you dress and the way you live." Today, my personal fashion choice includes my steadfast Carhartt coat. It is much like I am...old, a little tattered, holes sewn closed with thread, more than somewhat worn, but sturdy, highly wearable, comfortable, functional, AND.... a sure statement of who I am and wish to be.

I am now at the place where I could buy a new coat for working outside and I have other nice ones, but this coat – this rugged old ranch coat, stitched together at torn parts with duct tape wrapped around the zipper-pull and I have been through a lot together. The item seems to be gender-less but it has an air of ethereal romance of rugged days gone by. I find that I can be myself in this jacket. No pretense, no expectation, but a sense that I can handle myself in whatever comes along.

This coat stands against the cold, grows old rather gracefully, and holds its shape from day to day. *This* is the "me" to which I aspire. Max Lerner writes, "the turning point in the process of growing up is when you discover the core of strength within you that survives all hurt." I hope I am more like my old Carhartt every day.

The true ordeal, I believe, has been the experience of going from a three-dimensional world before the encounter to that of a two-dimensional existence. It does indeed have to do with one's spiritual life and belief systems. **Not to mention character.** Riding this decade after my encounter has briefed me in the domain of a feeling of lack-luster continuity. Just maybe that is the oddball crux of the engaging process – minus the emotional turmoil and extreme anxiety. I am finally looking at myself and the future. If not the **future exactly**, how I might *live* outside the realm of that experience.

Romance in a partnership is not something I any longer seek. The idea of growing old with someone remains beautiful, but feels a bit out of range at this stage of the game. Not so much because of age as due to the knowledge that I don't wish to take care of a man now. The long haul of developing a relationship tumbles on any emotional wish list.

My two adult daughters are now married with children and extended families. Working at NOT becoming my mother, my hope exists to offer support in the form of love and "hang in there" pep talks. The grass isn't greener or even better somewhere else, simply different...with dissimilar weeds.

It is not my intention to suggest that harmfully navigating personalities have ceased to exist. My focus now dances hesitantly with the idea that I can make something of a difference.

Moving back into a 3-D dimension from the fuzzy gray life of forever walking a tightrope subsists as a bizarrely tortuous trek. The heavily unrelenting narcissism of that *presence* in the past had become my world. Even the aftermath held the being as the axis of existence. Just like the ghost which haunts someone following a tragedy, I became the ghost in my own story, replaying the events and evaluations in endless loops. My beliefs now have found some embers still warm in the ashes. I believe that I must not only embrace possibility, but buttress that with a cord of gusto. Sometimes easier said than done. Uncertainty is also alive. Even **feeling** this doubt at times, it now appears true to me that a scheme of choice exists and that I am – to a very great part – in charge of my life fancies.   **The trick, of course, is to *choose well***.

I am told that I no longer possess a poker face. I can hose down, dress in something nice, even carry on a rather high-brow conversation, and although I don't prove an embarrassment, neither do I sparkle and shine...but I am hoping to get there. I feel a little like a character that might be played by Clint Eastwood. "You should never give up your inner self." Heavy sigh...a saddle bag with eyes.

Although many years have passed, I just recently discovered that I am finally ready to take myself as I am. There is a positive conclusion. I **can** let go. In the initial period within the wake of this runaway speedboat, I sought some kind of answer and explanations. Still I looked at *the other entity. Living in the past holds one firmly in a state of limbo.* And it doesn't matter how clearly one acknowledges this from an academic perspective. The series of gradual changes develop like coursework – one step builds upon another in knowledge and awareness.

I watched the movie, "Contact," again. Jodi Foster as the scientist Ellie, carries the energy of such an amazing quest for contact and catapults the viewer into the search along with her. The book by Carl Sagan concludes with Ellie's realization that intelligence is built into the universe itself. The movie closes on the idea of faith in possibilities. With an absence of tangible evidence, her experience with the alien encounter requires a leap of faith. Our heroine states that the brief communication left her with shining wonder and utter joy at life's prospects and forever changed her. The ordeal with a narcissist/psychopath does much the same. Although darker initially the potency of growth exudes a radiance of awareness. Life may not be as we all imagined but that doesn't make it less amazing.

This has also been my state of knowledge. The totality of learning within the obstacles posed by my ordeal provides certainty that **I am not a precipitate of these events. I am free.** My own contact was personal and with myself...along with my beliefs about this universe. There exists a rightness about this activity of living with a character of decency that we must actively elect.

Just as in a movie, let me flash back in time to share my drama. I watched an interview with the actor, Jason Beghe, about his departure from Scientology and his experiences within the organization. He has a keen intellect and marvelous compassion.

Even with these assets, he was still assessing just what happened and found much of the internal mulling hard to articulate. That is what living with an entity on the continuum of narcissism to psychopathy is like.

If we live in a hologram as scientists suggest is possible, I suspect it isn't they that are the rogue program, but we ourselves.

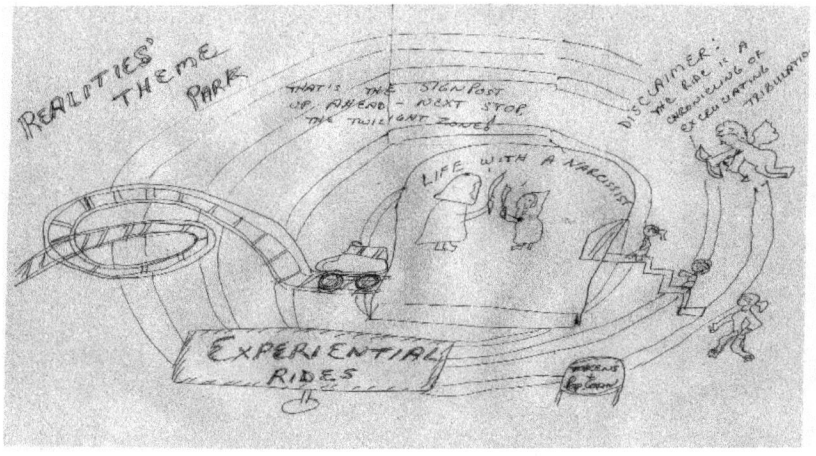

My drawing as I tried to understand my strange experience.

The farther away from the tumult and methodologies of me-me-me within the clan, I began to reclaim the essence of myself. Brainwashing and my own ideas of "continuing" until I made something workable out of the ordeal kept me trapped in a forever looping condition. I had created my very own ruse and deception of life. My existence became something of an autopilot program...and I genuinely felt there was no option. The dynamics of my thinking patterns had altered.

The next portion is the text of my book, *Romance Stew*. I was light-hearted and a bit naive. I think of Helen Keller's learning curve.

"I've reached that age where my brain went from 'you probably shouldn't say that,' to 'what the Hell, let's see what happens.' "
~ Facebook...ah, social networking

4

ROMANCE STEW

My personal search for meaningful relationships began with the quest for romance. Romance implied closeness or sharing, as well as intimacy. This closeness as in "true friendship" seemed to have priority over all other values when seeking the right romantic short- or long-term encounters.

In the right climate and under the right circumstances, we humans seem to have an instinctive generosity of spirit and willingness to share ourselves with others. It is a well-known spiritual and natural truth that when we reach out to others, we expand our own horizons and start living on a much grander scale.

My own family is an example of such loving and sharing. I feel blessed to have two daughters who are strong, independent, generous, compassionate, and intelligent. My brother is another example of a person who demonstrates integrity and honor in his interaction with others. My parents, now deceased, added to my personal growth by teaching me about making responsible choices – perhaps as much from the downward spiral of violent alcoholism as from their intrinsic values exhibited in sober times. They also imparted their wisdom concerning loyalty, faith and other virtues aligned with what I like to call universal or spiritual laws. These laws are the basis for world religions yet transcend any particular doctrine or creed. Like almost all families, we have seen the best and the worst of times.

It seems to be part of our life journey; how else could we learn except by inviting experiences into our lives that require choices? Trial and error is our best teacher! When success is measured not by the dollar sign but by personal achievements that include overcoming obstacles, our family could certainly stand tall. By the same token, we've also made grave errors in judgment that led to temporary chaos and despair. Yet through it all, we managed to stay focused on positive, clearly defined goals. Also inherent in the fabric of our family spirit was a sense of optimism.

Although self-help and inspirational material on relationships are readily available in every possible media format – books, CDs, DVDs, seminars, etc., and there's no shortage of life coaches and seminar trainers, for the most part I've discovered these programs disconcerting. I suspect their popularity is the ease with which they give us the illusion that we have already achieved those lofty goals ourselves, when in fact we are only vicariously experiencing the success of others. We Americans are all too willing to let someone else do the work for us.

That is why I decided to write this book. It has been my personal experience—and what better teacher can there be but the bruises and scratches from our own life's catwalk – that whatever our needs, whatever our desires — regardless of how much wisdom we've culled from others — **ultimately we have to do that work ourselves, our way!**

Each of us is unique; our lives are unique. We can read and listen to and attend seminars all our lives and still never make those important changes unless we customize the program for ourselves, and then *act on our intentions.* We also need to find a path of service that suits our own calling and connection to the God Source. In the large variety of life experiences, it is a given fact that happiness comes from focusing on answers and outcomes; as they say, we are part of the solution. Added to this piece of wisdom is humor, lots of it—

and I wish to share a bit of it with you here.

Recently, I have required dentures. It's amazing how this alters your idea of being attractive! Learning how to eat and speak all over again is enough to have to deal with, so I certainly wouldn't have a clue about the logistics of a passionate kiss! Maybe that will come in the future. Replacing one loss with another, recently I have started to add girth to what was once a svelte and shapely form. But do you know what? That's just fine, too! Who am I looking for? A 24-year-old Adonis with every hair and tooth still intact? Let's be realistic!

In fact, everything's just fine as long we stay true to who we are with the optimism of a romantic, and we're always cooking up another Stew . . . My concoction deals with me, a light-hearted soul, entering the strange world of life with a man lying on the continuum of narcissism to psychopathy.

I am my own special creation . . . I don't want praise, I don't want pity . . . I bang my own drum, some think it's noise, I think it's pretty . . . Why not try to see things from a different angle . . . What I am needs no excuses . . . Your life is a sham until you can stand up and shout, "I am what I am!"

~La Cage aux Follies

I have always felt that we are in direct communication with the author when we curl up with their book, or these days, when we connect with them through CD or PC. It is my hope that in sharing with you some of my feelings and thoughts on the subject of romance, I establish such rapport with you. May these ponderings make it easier for you to find answers to your own quest for romance, and also let you know that you are not alone.

It will be enjoyable to mentally sit together like two old friends and chat about our relationships. In my family we used the kitchen table as a place for brainstorming, sharing aspirations, and enjoying meals created by our Southern mother.

Whether the times were affluent or strained, Mom could always take a hodge-podge of ingredients and magically

whip up a savory stew. The pungent aroma of that simmering pot would literally fill the house. It seemed natural that Mom's stews would become our symbol of sharing, and mealtime and the kitchen table as our safety zone for venting as well as expressing new ideas.

Even during those "down times" – the negativity and enabling behaviors that inevitably accompany alcoholism
– we still managed to keep our balance. Then in later years during their recovery process, Mom continued this family tradition of the kitchen "round table" and we had a chance to partake in another type of growth experience. Just as in the myth of Camelot, we strove to start with ourselves to make a difference. Our topics had no boundaries and by the end of one of those talks, although we felt we may not have solved all the world's problems, we had surely rediscovered a little bit more about ourselves.

Be Open and Willing

Openness was a primary ingredient in these kitchen table discussions. Therefore, in this exchange, I want to follow that tradition as I expose my own personality, to support the belief that it's okay to freely discuss personal matters with others . . . especially when we are looking for self- fulfillment and self-discipline. Be free;

be open!

Like many others, my desire to find the right partner has elicited many of my idiosyncrasies. On several
occasions, the ensuing experiences have pointed to the need for my own growth and maturity. Does that sound like something that has happened to you as well? Perhaps it is "American" or democratic to let it all hang out, as they say; and in the process, look for romantic partners who are just as fearless.

As I look over my thoughts and New Age ideas of this period, I recognize my naivety about the 12% of the not-so-normal population that I would encounter with my marriage of later life. Populations hold variety.

America seems to be a culture ripe for interaction as well as candor. Even with all the hardships and global concern, one still feels a spirit of freedom or liberation as well as hope and a faith in a greater tomorrow. Emmet Fox writes that hope is the weaker sister to faith because faith demands certainty in our connection to a grander source of love and power.

My own personal goal is to "be the best self I can be," and that includes a built-in sense of goodness and empathy for others. I am grateful for the existence of a large number of counselors, healers and other professionals who can show us how to have a healthy and productive lifestyle, but as I pointed out earlier, ultimately it is up to us to determine how we want to fashion our lives and which choices we want to make.

External preoccupations or distractions as well as machines, devices, books, manuals, seminars etc. often present the illusion of doing that Inner Work, when we really aren't. If we stop for a moment to ask ourselves where we're going with all these activities, we may even be able to have a good laugh about the games of dodge ball and hide-and-seek that we play with ourselves.

Another virtue or characteristic of being American is that feeling or perception of being free to make our own choices when in truth we too readily allow therapists and other practitioners to "cure" or "heal" us, or improve our lots in life . It seems to go with a fast-food, fast-paced lifestyle.

The ability to take risks without expecting every encounter to work out is the most important ingredient for preparing any romantic stew. We must also be candid enough to accept ourselves in the eyes of others, warts and all. Obviously this requires a sense of humor as well as the ability to recognize that we are all perfect in the eyes of God . . . that no person is more perfect than another.

Each of us is a work in progress, and romance has very little to do with statistics: Number 10 body, IQ, credit rating, suntan, material possessions (home/ car/boat, computers and electronics), etc., etc. One can easily be swayed by the media and marketplace of athletic heroes and movie stars.

Today's women are hardly passive stay-at-home creatures willing to close their ears and eyes and let their husbands have a few on the side – without doing the same themselves! Today most women perform multiple roles in almost every type of coupling relationship. This has created a dichotomy to the point where time management can be a major challenge. Job, home, family, health maintenance, social life and extracurricular activities integrally linked to one's profession can push even the gentlest of women to the edge – physically, emotionally, mentally and spiritually. Add to this mix sleep deprivation and a house full of sick kids, and romance seems like something that exists on another planet.

The 21st century multi-tiered and taxed lifestyle has spawned a need to create a new paradigm for happiness and self-fulfillment – and perhaps a new format for romance. That seems like a big assignment and perhaps an impossible one.

Yet nothing else in our lives has stood still, so why should we romantics be frozen in time? What used to be traditional romantic protocol has disappeared along with Marcel perms, girdles, hats, and gloves. In this Global Information Age we may know the names of a whole batch of friends in Taiwan, Johannesburg, Brisbane and Madrid and be clueless about who lives next door. Our houses have no front porches and the corner grocery is now a franchised shopping mall. SUVs and RVs are the symbol of a society constantly on the move. Instead of marrying the boy or girl next door or our high school sweetheart, we jet across the Atlantic or Pacific for yet another experience with a new and different specimen.

And that is exactly where I headed. Like a true modern day pioneer. I ventured out beyond the back yard and went....West, East, South, and North.

Wherever I pitched my tents turned out to be fertile territory. In the Southeast, the Deep south, I found courtesy and gentle traditions. In the Northern Midwest, I encountered the more stoic descendants of miners, many of Norwegian heritage. In the Southwest, I dipped into the emotional heat of the Latino/Hispanics. With much gusto I celebrated the ethnicity of America's great melting pot.

Ah–ha! The Internet!

Like many others seeking romance, the Internet turned out to be a virtual gold mine of untapped potential. Risk was everywhere, and so was adventure. Automatic "pick and choose" lottery games turned out to be the most fun of all, but of course delivered the highest risk. Behind the veil of copious emails one can voice hopes and dreams that might never be shared should we meet in person - especially if we perceive the "stakes are high" and we don't want to disappoint or be disappointed.

We can also choose to be as romantic as we wish, without destroying the essence of ambiguity and evasiveness – two important ingredients for any introductory experience on the Internet. We can be free with compassion, kindness, tenderness and even hint at forthcoming passion, knowing the recipient doesn't need to be Mr. or Ms. Right. But just in case, we've got our bases covered.

It seems interesting that women enjoy emails more than men, who appear to communicate more easily by phone. My mother's large Southern farm family met regularly, bringing spouses and children to enjoy the hospitality, food, and conversation, and I remember the humor among the men gathered on the front porch. At a certain point my grandfather would gesture toward the kitchen where the women and girls were chatting jovially: "Is anybody doing the listening in there?"

Both emails and phone contact allow for the privacy of unwashed face, unbrushed teeth, curlers, nightgown or none.

Although grand, it's all illusion.

Posted profiles on the Internet match sites can be

fascinating and of course deliberately misleading – which is part of the gamesmanship. I tend to go for profiles that stray from mere multiple choice "yeses and no's" or lists of adjectives. I like narratives with a flare that deliver personal experiences flavored with humor, pathos or deeds of

derring-do. This indicates there's a pulse and blood

actually circulating. Sometimes you just jump, and learn to fly on the way down.

Yet even then, the profile information is scant and leaves much to be desired. Each of us is so complex; how could

we expect to really "know" a person from just a questionnaire? We have our marvelous days and then those other times when we question everything – even who we are to ourselves! Perhaps that's the true value of family and friends we've grown up with; they've hung out with us long enough to know how to go with the ebb and flow of our moods and metamorphoses. At least, however, these Internet handshakes give us an idea of shared values and social styles of interaction. That's a healthy start.

Do You Really Want to Meet Another Photocopy of Yourself?

One cannot possibly expect another human being to fill every one of our needs or respond to *all* of our desires.

Yet Western culture focuses on individuality, and when we stop to think about it, we realize that our contemporary lifestyle, although rich with social interaction, is essentially a one-on-one type of existence. This means we almost set ourselves up for times when we feel lonely. A person, whose life is rich and full, has many

friends and a large variety of interests. If a Significant Other is included in this list, the health and strength of the relationship will probably depend on staying connected to these supplemental friends.

No two people are alike.

Here's another reality check for those who expect "instant success" or "instant matches" through Internet match websites: It takes time to build a relationship. It appears that many people who submit their profiles in order to match with like-minded friends and intimate partners are looking for an instant connection with a built-in history that closely resembles their own. How could this ever be the case, when each of us builds that personal history over time and through diverse circumstances?! Perfect synchronicity of belief systems and backgrounds is both unrealistic and unavailable.

I wouldn't be human if I hadn't been emotionally bruised a few times from some of these Internet match encounters. And yet, I'll be the first to tell you these experiences have been a terrific education. I'm grateful for each of these encounters; they have not only taught me about what I didn't want in a romantic relationship; they also showed me

how to be more discerning. And most important of all: the failures did not stop me from trying again.

Let me emphasize once again the importance of risk- taking.   How are you going to know the water is wet unless you jump in?

Here are two more pointers I've learned during my romantic quests:

- *It's okay to be who you are!!*
- *When you're desperate for romance, you will attract desperate energy . . . and we all know where that leads.*

Recently I re-read *I Could Do ANYTHING if I Only Knew*

What It Was, by Barbara Sher. This book hits home. She writes that many of us have "real first targets" like "finding love or romance." We must permit ourselves to go after these desires because that is a huge part of who we are; it is also the greatest part of ourselves that we want to present to others.

Also, even if we desire to search for this *unique love*, it is important for *us* to have a strong secondary goal, such as an entrepreneurial venture, career or family. These secondary goals add dimension to our life. We become interesting people through what we find interesting.

"You'll never truly know how damaged a person is until you try to love them" ~ Unknown

5
COMMITMENT

This way of looking at myself and at my life has given me the permission to focus on what I am all about at the same time I am seeking romance. Soon we discover that when meeting someone, these two aspects of ourselves are integrally related – and then the magic begins. Our romantic connections also become healthy because they are not merely based on sexual satisfaction or temporary entertainment. Positive values and outlooks, a "destiny path" and set of goals, form the basis for any lasting relationship

. . . yet without romance, they lack that extra octane. You can feel the enthusiasm from anyone who has both!

" Commitment "

Okay, I just used the big word that scares away so many men – and these days, women as well – from forming any type of relationship at all. Of course, we're frightened

– that's part of taking risks! And "what if" it doesn't work out especially if children are already involved?

I'm the kind of person who needs commitment, especially when sex is involved. Lust is grand; those rampaging hormones are the best reminder we have about the

power and beauty of the life force energy. But when you add that radiance that comes from "true love" and appreciation, you have an unbeatable set of ingredients for a delicious Romantic Stew.

Ayn Rand suggests that love and sex in a relationship that includes intimacy, are our response to our highest values. ". . . sex is not the cause, but an effect and an expression of a man's sense of his own value."

Granted, these ideas expressed in *Atlas Shrugged* are based on experiences with men in the upper echelons of power. Yet, should that really make a difference? Is this not a universal principle that can be applied to all significant relationships? Power is a state of awareness and comfort.

I'm not suggesting that sexual enjoyment should be considered secondary or devalued in any way. It is – and should be – an integral part of that stew. The problem only arises when people believe the sexual act itself is a full representation of love – or one might even say, that sex alone is *any* significant representation of love. Expectations and ideas of right and wrong are sourced from this misunderstanding. Let the sex be the spices and herbs; let it be tenderizing ingredients. But the "meat, vegetables and potatoes" of a love relationship should be a deep and lasting friendship that consists of trust, honor, respect, lots of laughter and shared experiences of growth.

In spite of the limitations of "virtual matching," almost inevitably it broadens a person's horizons and alters their perspectives. Also, whatever the outcome from these connections, this renewed zest flavored with hope and desire will unconsciously be transported to other areas of our life.

The final test is of course, "reality" itself and not a computer screen. As we move beyond merely seeking romantic

partnerships and set our stakes still higher, in the process we will learn to more actively define ourselves and elicit similar qualities from another. There's something magical about this mirrored process.

Openness and excitement about the surprises every day may

bring are two wonderful gifts that are available to everyone. If

we add to this the decision to live in the NOW, we will always be fertile for connecting with like- minded (romantic) partners.

Dangers and Risks

Expect to find all types of people when you go on this romantic quest. The most common misfit will be someone who is not totally up-front about themselves. Also, you may find people with serious personality disorders. This isn't a "danger, danger, Will Robinson" warning, however. If your search is mainly through the Internet, do remind yourself that writing is only one method of communication. Just seeing data in print doesn't necessarily make it so.

Romance by its very nature is illusory. It is *intended* to be an invitation to the land of make-believe! This is an introduction. When we engage in our fantasies, we deliberately remove ourselves from the usual hubbub of daily activities with all its mundane chores, and enter into this exciting world of Oz where the streets are emerald green and every man and woman is a king and queen

. . . a bit of wizardry going on here? Why not? How does it make you feel? Romance is also "a moment" with a

place and time all its own; "real life" will still be bathing the baby or scrubbing the lasagna pan.

Romance is stupendous and can be glorious, but we all must learn to read others well... It is easy to fall into your own concocted story.

SirGalahadisStillinStyle

If you are a romantic, you will want to include plenty of old-fashioned courtesy and etiquette in your romantic stew. How gallant it is for a woman to be treated like a princess, and for a man to be treated like a combination of characters portrayed by Gene Hackman, Clint Eastwood and Harrison Ford, with a little Albert Einstein, Ralph Waldo Emerson and Abraham Lincoln thrown in for good measure! Even if these are not your favorite heroes, you get the picture. Remember: all of us look at our particular niche in reality through a veil of perception, and we select our choices according to our own wishes and needs.

Three of my own romantic encounters illustrate a time when, in my forties I was seeking a long-term commitment. This meant that new ingredients in my grocery list needed to be included when I set out to do my shopping.

Although in each of these relationships I

experienced some magnificent moments of what could really be called "love" as well as romance, the greatest gifts I came away with were those least expected.

In each of these relationships, I learned so much about *myself*! As each of these love fests became more intense and I became more passionately involved, it soon became evident to me that I was wobbling when it came to my core beliefs and values. I started questioning many things I had taken for granted or had just accepted almost pas- sively. The world started to look different; I discovered that *I was acting differently* with these men. What was the attraction? It was time for each of the relationships to end, since I couldn't imagine spending the rest of my life with either of them.

I was resolute, and grateful that I had the courage to walk away. That isn't to say I was less than painfully disappointed in the failure of these relationships to produce a long-term commitment. We all experience times when we fall down; The real trick is to get up and keep going.

There are still meals to prepare, dishes to wash, beds to make, etc. – and after a bit of healing, yet another person waiting in the wings! We are all ordinary people, but we don't have to be, if we allow ourselves to use our imagination, not every so often, but *all the time.* Each of us is an artist. We can paint the ethereal and highly fabricated landscape of "romance" as the background of every moment of our lives. Romance

can be a song that we hum while pushing the vacuum or picking up the kids after soccer practice. It is the music that touches us and makes us feel at one with a Source larger and greater than ourselves.

This is one of my favorite parables that came to my email box from Christian Godefroy, whose website is

www.club-positif.com.

A water bearer in India had two large pots, each hung on each end of a pole which he carried across his neck. One of the pots had a crack in it, and while the other pot was perfect and always delivered a full portion of water at the end of the long walk from the stream to the master's house, the cracked pot arrived only half-full.

For a full 2 years, this went on daily, with the bearer delivering only one-and-a-half pots full of water in his master's house. Of course, the perfect pot was proud of its accomplishments, perfect to the end for which it was made.

But the poor cracked pot was ashamed of its own imperfection, and miserable that it was able to accomplish only half of what it had been made to do.

After two years of what it perceived to be a bitter failure, it spoke to the water bearer one day by the stream. "I am ashamed of myself, and I want to apologize to you."

"Why?" asked the bearer. "What are you ashamed of?"

"I have been able, for these past two years, to deliver only half my load because this crack in my side causes water to leak out all the way back to your master's house. Because of my flaws, you have to do all of this work, and you don't get full value from your efforts," the pot said.

The water bearer felt sorry for the old cracked pot, and in his compassion he said, "As we return to the master's house, I want you to notice the beautiful flowers along the path."

Indeed as they went up the hill, the old cracked pot took notice of the sun warming the beautiful wild flowers on the side of the path and this cheered it some. But at the end of the trail, it still felt bad because it had leaked out half its load, and so again it apologized to the bearer for its failure.

The bearer said to the pot, "Did you notice that there were flowers only on YOUR side of your path, but not on the other pot's side? That's because I have always known about your flaw, and I took advantage of it. I planted flower seeds on your side of the path, and every day while we walk back from the stream, you've watered them.

For two years I have been able to pick these beautiful flowers to decorate my master's table. Without you being just the way you are, he would not have this beauty to grace his house."

Moral: Each of us has our own unique flaws. We're all cracked pots.

Some of us don't grow old gracefully, some are not so

smart, some are tall, large and big, some bald, some physically challenged, but it's the cracks and flaws we each have that make our lives together so very interesting and rewarding.

Live and love passionately, and in the process be kind to yourself and others.

"Make today worth remembering." ~ Steve Maraboli

6

SIMMERING ENTHUSIASM

In the quest for learning "to be" and to express myself, have found romantic relationships to be one of my best teachers. These romantic liaisons helped to define my sense of self as well as partnership. They also opened me to a new awareness about love as The Grand Adventure. I can certainly confirm that each of my romantic relationships was exactly that!

As vivid explorations of passion, they opened new landscapes portraying the vastness of life and splendor of the human heart. When we can love in the face of possible loss, heartache and disappointment and feel exhilarated about one's faith in "always something more around the corner," we begin to know and understand at a deeper level our Cosmic or God/Universal connection to All That Is and Is To Be. We discover that at any moment in life, we can choose to make a difference.

Although love needn't be linked with romance, unquestionably it has proven to be an exceptional pathway to "coming of age" for my own self-awareness.

As Tony Robbins says, "life should be lived with passion." In terms of finding a significant other, maybe all of us dyed-in- the-wool romantics aren't really looking for a way to merge with another but rather a way to seek our own self-fulfillment. Included in that quest is the courage to be ourselves at all times – to face obstacles head-on and find solutions ourselves, rather than relying on others. Isn't that the irony of it all?!! To strive to be together with someone in order to be totally independent and "a- lone." Perhaps we should say "a-lion," in the light of what it takes to have such fortitude!

Another paradox worth mentioning is the fact that it not only takes a village to raise a child; it also takes a "village" to maintain the health, vitality, and longevity of a relationship. To be an authentic learning tool, we have to incorporate personal ethics and an awareness of the effects of our behaviors on others. We need agreements and we want to be reassured that "the grass isn't always greener" elsewhere. We must also be aware of possible rocks on the path. Learning to share with another human being in a dynamic _

and by its very nature, romantic relationship is

bound to be filled with joy – and misunderstandings. As we attempt to set our own boundaries and as the closeness

develops into the type of intimacy that requires intervention and intermingling, we discover all sorts of hidden mysteries about each other that when brought to light, require exploration as well as definition. What a great learning experience this provides! Just when we think we might as well throw in the towel on the realities of a romance that

just isn't working and doesn't seem to have any promise, to the rescue comes that essence called faith. Lurking in the shadows is that one insight or incident that delivers the message that the relationship only needs time to meld together those already identified ingredients that are both positive and promising. Let it simmer; let it tenderize – and let the tears run together.

Communication is a marvelous link with another,

Be selective and stay in the NOW. No one has to know all the details of your past; and the truth is, they don't want to. In *Illusions*, Richard Bach writes, "The original sin is to limit the IS. Don't."

Admittedly, my own most cherished partners in this adventure of seeking romance have not always been the proverbial knight in shining armor. Like myself, they are vulnerable, with their own agendas. With each, the ecstasy was memorable... and so was the pain. In that wonderful film, *Something's Gotta Give*, the heroine, learning of her great love's desire not to make a commitment of monogamy, sobs   uncontrollably in fits of utter despair. But instead of going down the tubes and disappearing altogether, like any true romantic, she picks herself up, shakes herself off as if what she had just witnessed was nothing but a bad dream, and once more reaches into her heart to start creating yet

another "new life" for herself. Surely it is never long before the next Galahad comes riding along (substitute a man in his forties, slightly balding who sells insurance and had three bad marriages already, etc., etc.). Isn't life grand?

Although no one can tell anyone else "how to" find their way, we can at least communicate warmth and an attitude of camaraderie. "Hang in there!" Everything is really going to work out – even if he *did* tell you there's another woman in his life or he will never divorce his wife. Pitch that box of emails in the trash and start over.

Sharing is a way of elevating oneself and others to perceive life experiences from a more satisfying level. What you bring to reality is your spiritual presence . . . and that is no small parcel. Accepting yourself for all the past replays that cause guilt, shame, regret and a host of other emotions that bring on that familiar ache in the gut should not continue to recur if you dump all the baggage and stay focused on today, and NOW. Then you can start all over with that new friend on the block called "the best you can be."

Life is about choices. Don't limit your options or opportunities!

INSTRUCTIONS FOR LIFE FROM THE DALAI LAMA

Take into account that great love and great achievement involve great risk...

- When you lose, you don't lose the lesson...
- Remember that not getting what you want is sometimes a wonderful stroke of luck...
- Learn the rules so you know how to break them properly...
- Judge your success by what you had to give up in order to get it ... AND
- Approach love and cooking with reckless abandon.

I entered my own adulthood with many of the same excesses that are noted in Robin Norwood's *Women Who Love Too Much.*

Much of my time was spent searching for compatibility in relationships. The journey over treacherous terrain, with a lengthy evaluation of my own responsibilities, has brought me to acknowledge patterns learned in a household of violent alcoholism. Later, my uncle introduced me to, or perhaps submerged me in, Scientology.

This experience with its cult mentality, offers far worse properties of alienation by deliberately using intellectual awareness as a tool for hiding one's imperfections. By being candid and open in what was known as "processing," I allowed myself to be on the receiving end of denigrating techniques geared toward altering my perceptions of right and wrong. What an important learning experience that was! It was also an eye-opener when it came to evaluating potential romantic relationships.

By examining my fears and learning from the mistakes of those who have chosen such negative, limiting and highly stressful environments, I have become so much more discerning... hmm, or so I thought. I have also been delivered from inhibitions that are part of this roller coaster ride of substance as well as cult leader dependencies.

Self-acceptance and a place in the grander scheme of things will be your rewards . . . You will also rekindle your joy, sense of humor and compassion for others who are caught in those webs from which you have freed yourself.

A line from the movie, *Romancing the Stone*,

seems an appropriate description of my outlook concerning the quest for a romantic partner: "I'm not a hopeless romantic; I'm hopeful." Instead of trying to find that man who can be all the qualities you seek in a partner – ethical, strong, self-aware, compassionate, and bright – strive to develop these qualities in yourself. Be honest with yourself, and enjoy your worthiness.

Reinforcing my thoughts on the subject of self-empowerment and personal growth are part of the shopping list in Barbara Mohr's book, *The Cosmic Ordering Service,* as well as Phil McGraw's *Self Matters*, Esther and Jerry Hicks' *The Amazing Power of Deliberate Intent*, Shakespeare's *Much Ado about Nothing*, and films such as *Must Love Dogs* and even *Dogma*.

Following is a brief recap of the last few years of my ever-so-slow growth, a quote from the Max Ehrmann poem, "Desiderata" comes to mind:

Be yourself.

Especially, do not feign affection.

Neither be cynical about love;
for in the face of all aridity and disenchantment
it is as perennial as the grass.

My own case was one of a bit of masked desperation in the search for acceptance. In hindsight, I know I am hard on myself. I'm certain others can be just as uncompromising when it comes to knowing when we are operating with facades.

I told a male acquaintance that I thought my most recent connection with a gentleman I had come to like and with whom I'd engaged in online hopes of intimacy, may have collapsed. His response, although a tad crudely expressed, was actually one of kindness.

He suggested that I should enjoy sex only when needed.

This response clearly defined the distinctions

between male and female needs!

Even in real life, the erotic side of a committed

Love

relationship is only momentary expression of the depth of a union with mutual goals and a future road map. Sometimes we forget that this whirl of excitement reflects more than mere animal magnetism.

A cross the Gap" – A Parody of Hopefulness

It was the end of summer and already cold here in Montana. Soon it would once again be snowing. It was that time of year when she loved to be inside, cozied up by the fire, her head nuzzled in the lap of a lover . . . She was seated

at her computer, totally absorbed in responding

to an email, when suddenly

she felt his arms circling her shoulders. Quickly he swiveled her around to face him; cupping her chin in his hand, he kissed her sweetly at first, and then, as she began to respond, more deeply, with greater passion. At once her body was on fire, the flame of his lips igniting her expectation. As he withdrew from her, his mouth curled upward in a tiny satisfied smile. He knew exactly the effect he created, and it was good. He liked that, for it also kindled his own fire.

The smell of him intoxicated her as once again he drew close and covered her mouth with his own, kissing her hungrily. She was already aching for his touch, and he knew it. Resting his hand lightly on her shoulder, slowly he moved downward with his fingers, lightly tracing the outline of her low-cut blouse. As they paused tentatively on the pulse of her neck, he felt her breath quicken then grow erratic. He knew what he wanted and he also knew she could not resist him much longer.

Taking her hand in his, he placed it where she could feel his mounting desire and held it there. He nuzzled her neck, covering it with slow, small deliberate kisses, his hands moving beneath the soft material of her blouse, unfastening her bra and slipping it away from her breasts. A barely audible sigh es- caped her as she moved against him and let herself be lifted up and carried to the bedroom.

Gently he lowered her onto the bed, already removing her clothes, at the same time getting naked himself. As he pulled her to him, he let his hand memorize every curve of her body. He knew women all right . . . knew exactly where it would feel best to have him touch and stroke and linger just long enough for the type of arousal that would cause her to surrender . . . but not yet. It was still too soon.

Now all she cared about was making sure he knew he was making her feel sexy and glamorous and most of all, desired. How she had longed for this moment ... for days, months, she had mentally choreographed   it . . . all she wanted was for him to show her just how special and remarkable she was.

She also knew she was inducing the same effect. Now he held her tightly while practicing all the techniques he knew would hold her captive . . . and when she gasped and begged him not to make her wait . . . but he persisted . . . now teasing her and driving her to even greater ecstasy . . . just when she thought she couldn't stand any more . . . stopping, then starting all over again, gentle at first and then demanding . .. it was as if they had been lovers forever, as if they had always known everything about each other.

It had been so long since she'd last felt love like this . . . Then as suddenly as it had begun, all movement ceased and they relaxed into each other .

. .

This little fantasy was of course, nothing more than that. At age 53 and momentarily without a partner, I found myself daydreaming about romance. My poor mother would be horrified at my erotic writings! Like most women of her generation, she was very strait-laced. *What kind of daughter did I raise*, she'd be wondering. Ha! If she only knew!

I did have a sense of balance, however. The hunger for romance was nicely controlled by the glut of

responsibility in raising two daughters almost wholly on my own. Integrating my own social activity with the propriety of acceptable standards for them was one of those remarkable juggling feats known only to single moms who enjoy adventure and will settle for nothing less than Authentic Romance. Obviously, such encounters can never take place within the confines of one's own residence and must be logistically planned to coordinate with the PTA bake sales, Girl Scout outings, piano lessons, meal planning and dropping off and picking up the dry cleaning. But I did it . . . successfully.

Fifty-three years old and here I was, writing border- line pornography; I looked in the mirror at the

aging woman staring back at me and my eyes crinkled as I started to chuckle at my own inimitable self. "*You romantic old devil, you!*"

Soon after I scripted that little ditty, a new man entered my life — and I might say, not a minute too soon! My appetite had been further whetted by two DVDs,

Someone Like You and *The Mirror has Two Faces* . . . Posting my profile on a couple of new Internet match sites, I put the fresh pot of romantic stew on the front burner and as it started to simmer, I could already smell its heady aroma wafting through my imagination . . .

In the initial emails between this latest fatal attraction, an actual connection didn't seem likely. First of all, an ocean divided us. One of my less desirable traits may be to eat when I'm hungry. I had little patience for long-term keyboard relationships.

Just at that time, I was gifted with an unexpected financial windfall and found myself contacting tour guides and bed & breakfasts for a trip overseas. This overseas outing was described to my deceased mother — whose face appeared in the shadows whenever I went to (an empty) bed at night — as cultural enrichment, a way to expand my horizons.

Would she have believed me? My real reason for the trip was to feed my lust and pray that he didn't have prostate problems or need Viagra.

My new virtual friend was charming if a bit quiet . . . nevertheless I could sense a drive and passion beneath the calm; and he was incredibly bright. That is ALWAYS a plus. On his resume he listed

IT expertise and military service. His apparent vitality coupled with the exotic flavor of a European Man made him deliciously "bigger

than life." The ethernet waves indicated an anxious heart and also that he really did like me.

I am no spring chicken, and at 53, most assuredly I would not be recruited for a head or body-shot on the front cover of any magazine except maybe a How to Clean Almost Anything catalog. I can most aptly be described as the "stay at home and be sloppily comfortable" in sweatshirt, jeans and tennis shoes type of gal. I am not and never have been a suited, heeled and heavily detailed office or corporate type. Short, somewhat stocky, with brown/black hair and golden brown eyes, I resemble the odd-ball

female in The Truth about Cats and Dogs. I don't think I need to say anything more.

On the brighter side, I like to think of myself as possessing intellect as well as keen evaluative skills. Those are valuable traits for any man, right?

As long as he senses no serious competition with himself and his ego, of course.

In the marriage department, however, I'd have to admit I'm a slow learner. With five failures to my debit, for some reason I seemed to keep hitting on the wrong formula, or the wrong men. Or maybe the "something wrong" was with me and not them. I hadn't figured that out yet, but at least I had a sense of humor about it, and hadn't given up.

Believe it or not, in spite of all these escapades and my determination to keep my mother's ghost locked in the

closet, my life for the most part was rather humdrum and dull. Of course, even the ordinary has its rewards; I have two wonderful daughters.

It was the first time since I'd engaged in Internet matching that *I* did not initiate the contact; *he did*! I can't begin to tell you how many tally points that automatically put in his corner. Usually I was asked by my potential "matches" to make a list of questions (ingredients for the stew?) and   send it

to them so I could learn more about them. Didn't they have enough originality in them to write that list themselves, I often wondered. This method of breaking the ice seemed totally unromantic too left-brained and logical.

I was enchanted and immediately charmed to be approached by a conversationally-adept man of maturity who was actually able to write a complete sentence that was both clever and
literary! I was virtually mega- bitten and smitten already.

Months of emails and telephone calls had fleshed him out a bit more, or at least as much as possible with the ocean still dividing us. His photos depicted a tall, ruggedly handsome man definitely of Irish heritage as I was. The expression in his eyes and the way his mouth curved ever so slightly upward, indicated he had not only experienced a full life but had come through it "safe and sane." There's much to be said for that alone. His conversational skills were comfortable, smooth, and oozing masculinity with an Irish lilt. He was the essence of humor and charm. I was also reading "integrity, strength, easily shared views and   business acumen."

Oops...the white knight syndrome was creeping up on

me. Of course, I was curious about why he had contacted an American woman if everyday, physical fore-plan, interplay and post-play was on his "to do" list.

However, in one of his phone calls, he had provided a ready response to my query. He'd simply entered the "search" profile generically without specifying a location for the woman of his dreams.

One hears all sorts of stories about Internet match- ing, and you really have two choices. You can listen with both ears wide open or you can refuse to listen and en joy the risks. I had chosen the second.

I was ready for the ultimate test. It was time to dry up that ocean or learn to walk on water. I told myself if I booked the flight I would be doing it only to participate in

a chemistry experiment, i.e., to see if my raging hormones were simply mind-induced or if there was some actual juice behind all this *sturm und drung*.

It had come to the point where brief phone conversations and even copious emails would never suffice or supplant mouth-to-mouth resuscitation. The only benefit I could determine for staying in this holding pattern was to give my romantic illusions enough time to grow into a full-length porno piece (who knows? Maybe I could even find a publisher). In other words, I could continue being Cleopatra in my jeans and sweatshirt without mascara, earrings or uncomfortable shoes, or take

the bull by the horns and buy that plane ticket.

This argument was far from convincing. Sometimes we'll even sacrifice being ourselves in order to meet that Prince Charming.

We made plans to meet. I got my passport and checked on all the overseas flights. I told my friends and family, contacted employment prospects overseas, and I was ready.

And if I haven't discussed this before, let me say right here, once and for all, that the Internet is only ether. Smoke and mirrors.

We had one thing in common: both of us believed in reality. In other words, if I'd shown up in my at-home uniform and he'd delivered himself as the doorman or faceless waiter that he was, both of us would have at least created enough spark to light a match. Wooden match, that is; not a his-and-her, she-and-he match.

After many times through the mill, I was still a believer, even though by now I'd realized the grass is the same

shade even in the desert where there is none. Different weeds.

I was impressed that *he* had sought me out first; it had been many a moon

since my howling had been silenced by a man's lips or anything else.

Taking the Plunge

Once more I was on the brink of something and about to fall in. Fantasies? The bumper sticker is right: "Real women don't have hot flashes... they have power surges!"

As I continued to strike out, one of my best friends, a gifted psychologist and psychic, would scold me gently, "You need to trust yourself. You don't have to fanaticize or superimpose your fantasy on the wrong man. Just let it happen, and it will!" Nice, but one has to be a bit careful in learning discernment.

Our long emailing and phoning marathon was moving forward, I thought – or at least it felt like commitment with possible marriage; after all, he had already broached that "maybe." However, my attempts to arrange for a meeting were met with the response that it was "bad timing."

That statement could have meant anything, of course ... and I didn't want to think the worst. I'd already been through that scene a few times, with men who seemed to enjoy bouquets of women simultaneously rather than a single flower, one at a time, as in marriage.

I was stymied . . . and yet the secretive air was mesmerizing. If I were writing a romance novel, it would almost be a necessary ingredient. Yet there was still a part of me that liked Reality. I wanted some type of expectation beyond tomorrow's email or the weekend phone call.

While cleaning files on the Internet match service where we had found each other, I happened to stumble upon his profile in the "active" list once more. Was that a coincidence or was Someone Upstairs (or Downstairs) trying to tell me something? When I casually mentioned this to him, he matter-of-factly answered that he was "no longer in the market."

That was a good answer, but not honestly the one I wanted to hear, because it didn't really seem to tell me what I wanted to know. Why was his profile still active? Soon after, however, it was, or at least *that* profile was removed. I say "that" profile because an unusual thought had suddenly popped into my head.

What was I sensing about this man, I wondered wild- ly. (What if, in fact, this website was part of a task force of sorts, to follow males who contact females posting profiles?) My imagination was now ...

as fertile as my appetite for romance. I proceeded

to make some inquiries into the type of female profile that would flag down such a task force and learned that she would probably fit my specs to a tee: someone relatively long-standing in a community, naturally quiet, economically stable and not particularly outstanding enough to raise eyebrows. If that is how I would be described, I can't say I was impressed, nor did I feel particularly desirable.

At that point, why didn't I simply "jump ship"? Perhaps because I want to believe that others are honorable, like I think myself to be.

Like a true romantic, I wanted this "maybe" to have a happy ending. The last marriage had left me feeling like leftover meatloaf.

I wasn't asking anyone to evaluate my psychological dependency issue; I needed a relationship because I was a romantic, and clearly this thing called love needed to be done by more than one human being. It was like a battery: positive and negative tips and ends that needed charging *together*.

The End...

Poof, just like that, it was gone. My Galahad simply evaporated as if he had been nothing more than a USB cable that had suddenly been yanked out of my virtual laptop.

What went wrong?

Maybe nothing except that there was nothing *to* go wrong. Ah, sweet mystery of life along with a bit of misery at the loss of this possibility.

I decided to take a respite from Internet matching, at least long enough to recover from the shock of –

well, nothing.

God loves a story, let us be the heroes of our own. — Marc Gafni

7

REACHING FOR FLAVOR
MORE IN TUNE WITH REALITY

Do you think the world is ready for an Erma Bombeck of the divorce crowd? I suppose with five marriages under my belt I could apply for the position. After so much failure, surely I had collected sufficient feelings of inadequacy to be able to laugh at myself.

The word failure means, "lack of success, an unfavorable outcome of a venture." I wonder if that is true of divorce in general, or maybe specifically as well. Universal laws exist which may be explained by the actions of cause and effect. We are accountable for our choices, and by accepting this responsibility, we own our behaviors and actions.

So what? If the marriage isn't good, it isn't good. It's a failure.

In former times, a woman stayed in a bad marriage

because it was her only means of survival. Today, however, woman is liberated. She now equally shares the burden of bringing home the bread and therefore is free to clean the home for making the bread *and* the bacon. Often a good deal of her time is spent at the courthouse trying to get her ex-spouse to pay child support. The era of Superwoman is here.

Remember the line in *Indiana Jones and the Last Crusade* when the villain, having chosen the wrong chalice from which to drink, dies horrendously . . . The knight matter-of-factly explains, "He chose poorly."

How could I be so positive and Pollyanna-ish not to be bitter? After all those vicissitudes that ended up in Delete & Trash, how could I still long for romance?

If only I were unique and authentically eccentric. No matter how I tried to be unusual, I still ended up with the same lofty ideas about perfect partnerships in which each strengthened the other, learned from the other, was nourished by the other – and both equally loved hot tubbing naked – together.

Why did I still love the idea of exploration – all types and forms of it? Isn't that what elevated the

status quo beyond McDonalds and Burger King?

Was I babbling, or what? Didn't I know the difference

between a good hamburger and a fast food one?

Unity; that's what I was after. Unity that provided accessibility of communication that served as a new platform for creation and that could simultaneously sustain the status quo of day to day living. God help me, I was starved for a man.

Let's try that again: if the dream exists for the format of a union, holds enough viable drive for its manifestation and can be guided with thought toward the best survival for both parties, the ripple-effect should prove beneficial for each person, the couple, and all the peripheral life forces touching upon that couple's relationship thereafter. We need not lose ourselves in statistics to become engaged in a partnership. Each individual brings unique qualities to the table and I strongly suspect that we women have not always been valued for the continuity, beauty, and structure that we supply, but more for that meat loaf, mashed potatoes and gravy, and of course home-baked apple pie, delivered shortly after he turns the handle on the front door. A la mode.

Of course, I have noted with some interest that in this struggle for feminist actualization, we may have lost some footing. "Just do it!" wears thin after awhile. Sole to sole, we need rubberizing and refurbishing at least once a month at the end of that period of "bitchiness."

Maybe romance is only a figment of the women's imagination and has nothing to do with men after all. Who are we, but roles? Professions, jobs, incomes and bra sizes. Do we not also possess souls, and do we not also think and feel like the persons we are supposed to be imitating? Do we not also have drive and overdrive like any good pick- up truck?

What should we of the unwed set, *do* to initiate contact with someone who might be just the right complement to who we think we are?

The saga continued with this delightful gentleman to whom I'd been introduced by a friend and local editor,

and perhaps I was the only one who wasn't surprised that I was still *virtually* falling in love. A meaty broth base of streaming emails thickened with countless phone calls

and the need to get a flat rate account for my phone service continued to whet my appetite.

Life was good; I was living on hope and continued to enjoy my fantasies of "the next step" which of

course would have to end at the altar if it was ever going to satisfy my full list of requirements.

We seemed to share the same philosophies; he seemed to have all the right vital signs. He might even share the housework, I hummed as I pushed the vacuum cleaner over the carpets and waited for his next email.

Finally we got to the point where we dropped our defenses, bared our souls and dived headfirst into Fragile Ideas. The net result was a lovely friendship rooted in mutual trust and respect. All we needed was "real time" and moments of physical intimacy, which finally materialized. Ah, sweet bliss! Even the chemistry was there as I'd hoped; my soul was singing!

This time the flaw that surfaced took me completely by surprise. Apparently Mr. Right was looking for a cross between Angelina Jolie and Jennifer Lopez – what was I thinking? – that a man who had brains and vital organs intact would be different from a Neanderthal? I was hurt that what he really wanted was someone to drape over

his arm and exhibit like a prize catch on some fishing expedition.

Who would have guessed that behind almost every
Wall Street Journal is the latest *Playboy*?

Have you ever been told you would be the perfect partner in every way, with just a little plastic surgery, like
on the face, breasts, waist and hips,
and . . . well, all over?

And what was I thinking? That this specimen was going to be different from the rest? Of course. And actually I may have been right. Another problem beneath the layers of apparent shallowness had suddenly emerged and seemed to be more related to what was going on.
Commitment...
What better excuse could Mr. Right who was slowly turning into Mr. Never, come up with, that would be convincing enough to

force me to back off because he was afraid to take the next step? How easy to insult *me* rather than face his own ineptitude!

Indeed, what better way to force a woman to back off than to tell she was, well, not ugly, but . . . well, not beautiful either.

It still hurt, and maybe for months longer than it should have . . . I had thought this was to be the

"real thing."

Although each of us slid to the point of forgiveness, this only released him to the next opportunity and

left me feeling miserable.... *Casablanca*'s script line of

surrender, "We'll always have Paris," seemed appropriate for the closure.

Another quote comes to mind: "A gate only works if a corral comes with it."

Next . . .

The man was charismatic to the hilt: street wise, strong and ex-military. Although I enjoyed the fantasy of the man-among-men with his go-it-alone attitude, it was more than that, I convinced myself. It was also the self- determination that seemed to come with the package that included service and some form of death-or-war related regimentation.

That was not the determining factor, however. More important than honor within a group was the military man's ability to handle his finances . . . not mine, his. I am well-equipped with the latest bookkeeping software that never seems to erase the minus signs and zeroes fast enough, mainly because too often in the past I have surrendered to loan requests delivered in compromised positions when saying no might ruin that lovely fictitious commitment.

I thought this ex-Army Ranger could well be the love-of-my-life.

Even though he told me he wanted to keep traveling (did that also mean "keep shopping" as well?) – we actually met and liked each other.

Do you remember the role Jack Nicholson played in *Something's Gotta Give*? If you do, the romantic stew that followed several months of this relationship will be flavored with even greater meaning.

Webster's definition for the word "relationship" in terms of a verb (to relate) is "to actively desire and cherish." Added to this is my Internet friend, Rebecca Brent's definition of love as "more than a feeling; it is a promise." (*Enchanted Spirit* e-zine)

In my quests for answers – and these always deal with who I am (or more accurately, who I choose to become) I have met the most charming, generous and delightful participants in this game called life. Marc Gafni, author of *Soul Prints*, talks about receiving soul prints from another. Gafni writes that biblical consciousness deals with the move from loneliness to loving, and that Kabalistic mystical knowledge regards the act of receiving as "the highest fulfillment of biblical vision." We want to share ourselves with others and to have them reciprocate. The ultimate fulfillment is to find the right match with like hearts and souls.

This *M*an from *N*ew York, *M*y ex-*A*rmy Ranger

His accent was Thick New York and he had all the makings of a delicious dish for any woman who is a connoisseur of culture. Add a dash of libertine spirit and it already seemed like an entrée fit for a queen.

It took courage to continue that oddly one-sided love, but then I told myself, did he not reflect that image of myself

that I so longed to become? He had made his way to my

door after reading some of my ideas on romance

submitted to an Internet post. He was simply and openly curious.

Forget the commitment with a man like this; clearly he could never be tied down by anyone. *No judgment, no evaluation, just take him as he comes. Openly express myself and enjoy the interactive video stream of all that would follow.*

Did he not understand and appreciate my sense of

humor and perspective on life? Exuding

animal magnetism, determination, additional animal magnetism, charm and yet more animal magnetism, he was just my type. Obviously his successes in life were closely linked to his high sex drive that spilled into all manner of conversation, gesture and body language. It was also exhibited in his diverse entrepreneurial endeavors. He was a comfortably wealthy man, or at least he professed to be.

The spark of danger I feel rippling from such a man is

exactly that level and degree of virility that makes me

believe the impossible. It is like a pheromone. Clearly a man of this ilk knows who he is and is enjoying every minute of that knowledge alone, as a bachelor. It had to be that way, or otherwise his partner might steal the limelight. What a shame. Seldom had I experienced such a high level of pure testosterone.

And yet, underneath all this bluff and gruff flowed a river of questions about his own reality and of course, the fear of opening up to another. What would be the consequences?

What is truth? What is illusion? Does anyone really know? Does anyone really even ask the question?

We women tend to give the benefit of the doubt to both truth and illusion, since it all comes out in the   wash.

Herein lies the dilemma. If I am to be a "relationship" person and a romantic one at that, how am I to experience such encounters if I don't allow myself the exuberance of Possibility?

How am I to ignore my heart's battle cry: *just let me give of myself without barriers that are supposed to protect me from ultimate pain. Oh! It hurts with such exquisite agony!*

By stopping short right before that important moment of consummation I felt I was wasting all that good material from that willing individual whose intention, after all, was to give it to me. Should I refuse such generosity and frustrate both of us?

It is this failure to have my own essence perceived and valued in such moments like these that causes the greatest conflict.

The montage of experience certainly had to have at least one New Yorker, so what did I have to lose? At least for

awhile. Because just as I predicted, he soon moved on to another and then another . . . and then another! Far too scary to stop long enough and ask himself who he was, and far better – and easier – to let him be defined by yet another female encounter.

Almost predictably, six months later, he returned to try to rekindle the flame. But by then I had already bought a new computer, revamped my cathartic writings and deleted his files along with the other rejections.

Taking his courage in my hands, however, reluctantly I agreed after another year had passed with our on again/ farewell again relationship, to embark yet again on another version of the same trek. Although I bought him a pair of slippers to take care of his cold feet, I should have known they wouldn't suffice in this pre-charted journey across the tundra.

He had written his own operational manual and once it had been published, I suppose he felt he had to stick to the rules. Business is business, and every good entrepreneur knows if you stray

across the boundaries laid out and carefully bullet-pointed, you run the risk of ruining the numbers and potential return on investment.

After we said good-bye to one another for the final time, I concluded it takes remarkable humility to accept the idea that each of us must be free to follow our own destiny, especially when all the threads of life's vast multi- dimensional web touch so many others. Somehow, we must access the memories of connectedness to know and feel that we are not alone with all this pain of rejection and fear.

Added to this necessity is awareness of that passionate heat that is experienced when we first recognize yet another candidate whose file must be transferred from the old computer that just crashed, to the new one that has not yet been fire-walled and secured against phishing and phashing.

I am reminded of the film, *The Never Ending Story,* in which Nothingness takes over and becomes reality.

Imagination and a desire to be "more than ever be- fore" restored that realm of illusion as grandly as if still within the parameters of love. Energy, drama, action and self-expression can be used to create any union that pretends to be love. And so, it is truly we who must acknowledge our own worth and find ways to take part of that love on a grander level even than the heightened displays of emotional

energy that were so exciting yet short-lived.

Soulmates

The crux of love between soulmates is the act of sharing without reservation. Implicit in lust and love is exploration of unknown territory, with gusto.

A promise must blossom in order to be strong enough to weather all storms. We must grow to honor each other together and hold that special someone tightly within the confines of our thoughts at all times and especially during those moments of compressed joy when the objective is to automatically let loose and fly . . . This organ of destiny is the one goalpost to whom we can cling, the one land- mark that is going to listen to our story with all its hu- man frailties, until we are finished weeping and wailing. We tell ourselves over and over that this is the one part of ourselves that is going to deliver happiness whenever we need it.

The loved one I am currently describing is that chosen being who is dearest to my heart; he is the person with whom each of us feels we are truly "seen," for it is this counterpart to ourselves that makes us feel like we are "home." With this being we can truly be ourselves, or at least the one we acknowledge to be *us* over all the other versions. Or at least we can say this much: it is the one we feel most comfortable portraying to the world.

The scene unfolds in my mind's eye, with all its melodrama. Veils of reality reflect my unobtrusive and seemingly passive nature in the mirror of this plane of existence. Underneath, however, a warrior rides the currents

of the "here and now." Unlike the presence seen by so

many outsiders, I radiate confidence, strength, self-determinism, and a ferocious courage.

Embodying the traits of the Dragon in Chinese Astrology, I long to share these hidden parts of me with a special love(r). I desire to shed the beliefs of this world and be just plain, me . . freely able to offer love in its many formats.

Let the sun shine through the clouds of deception even if it's already raining inside. Let my true identity be revealed and let it be massaged and cherished in the degree to which it craves to be exposed to that special "other."

I can personally attest to the fact that passion raises one from the point of ineffectual essence to a new presence of heightened direction. One can easily find that hunger to savor those special activities that spring from the fountainhead of life. Perhaps personal revelations occur only when we undergo that trial of "separation" just before we allow ourselves to give in. Do we not realize by now that *this* is part of the ultimate experience?

Part of the loss is in the gain . . . followed by the shared silence afterward.

Henri Bergson wrote: "to change is to mature; to mature is to go on creating oneself endlessly." If we apply this aphorism (which may or may not be true . I haven't yet decided) to romance and let it operate from a perspective of love, we will discover that our problems and surprises can be handled with warmth, non-judgment and compassion.

Added to this is the comfort from Emmet Fox's thoughts: "Fear is the absence of faith" (*Power through Constructive Thinking*). Unquestionably, it takes courage to risk and reach toward intimacy. Time and awareness also help.

Kahlil Gibran describes it best:

Love has no other desire but to fulfill itself . . . But if in your fear you would seek only love's peace and love's pleasure, Then it is better for you that you cover your nakedness and pass out of love's threshing-floor, Into the seasonless world where you shall laugh, But not all of your laughter, And weep, But not all of your tears.

What is in store for me next? I have no idea except that it's an adventure; a bit different this time because I am more aware of my connection to Universal Love and its laws. Am I still hopeful? Of course — even in the cold morning air. I feel, however, a bit more reserved these days, at least until tomorrow.

I did the usual whenever these feelings of normalcy overcome my usual adventuresome spirit: I have cleaned out the closets, rearranged furniture, and done some heavy-duty deep cleaning. I'm saying goodbye to SOMETHING

I felt was special. I'm not sure what that is yet, but it sounded good to write that down and read it over a few times myself as I share it simultaneously with readers.

However, in conclusion, I do know this: Love and even the romantic quest of it will always have a special place in my heart. This means I will never try to be reasonable or acceptable to anyone except myself and in the process, always see the best in others at the same time I recognize and acknowledge blatant neuroses as well as a large number of dysfunctional personalities . . . believing without reservation that this universe always was and will be a reflection of our own expectations. And if a key exists for creating a semblance of the life we desire, our own REFLECTION must be it.

What the Bleep Do We Know!? seems like a perfect description of what I have just iterated in my own words.

I am also working on being kind to myself, to be my own best partner in crime. After all, one cannot do any- thing corrupt to oneself without first laying out the plans and folding back the covers. So let it be said for all to hear: I'm ready, Universe, and ripe to once more begin my Quest!

And as I pull up to the Universe's drive-in window and

place my order ("Hold the onions") I feel a bit like the gal in the joke who finds a bottle with a genie inside: "I'm not the 3-wish kind of genie . . . you only get one wish, so

make it good . . ." OK. Deep breath. Here goes.

He will know himself. He will be warm and loving, strong but sensitive. He will have enough courage to be monogamous and won't care if I run up all his credit cards. He will even be trained to put down the toilet seat.

Of course, I'm just joking. I've learned by now (haven't I?)

that romance is so much more than a list. Who would be so foolish to try to pin it down or pin down any man for that matter? One day I stumbled across an old book by Stella Terrill Mann, *Change Your Life Through Love*, which sums my new awareness. One might call it the Trinity for

The Good Life, giving it a little religious flavor, if

you will: "In order to manifest a powerful life, first you have to have the desire and then you have to act on the desire." I might add that finally, you have to believe that the mess you've made in the process is truly yours.

In other words, own who and what you are, and pay the consequences. The love part is the underpinnings that will eventually be removed in order to reveal the essence in all its flesh and blood.

Thomas Mann says it even better:

But how are we to bring every desire, action, and belief under the law of good? First by establishing love as the highest law of our life . . .We create the conditions of our lives by our desires, actions, and beliefs. Our desire tells the creative force what it is we want it to

do. Our prayer, or request by word, deed, and thought, sets the force into motion to

produce that which we have desired. Our faith or belief is our mental acceptance of that which we have desired or ordered. When this has been done the law of creation has been complied with, and it is done unto us. . . . we must also learn to accept love. For love is the force which creates good. Its nature is to create more good than existed in the first place. Its purpose is to carry the beloved forever forward.

With the greater love, one is expanded into an understanding of life and the joy, which is ours by our decisions and willingness to act upon those in faith.

"There is no use trying," said Alice; "one can't believe impossible things."

"I dare say you haven't had much practice," said the Queen. "When I was your age, I always did it for half an hour a day. Why, sometimes I've believed as many as six impossible things before breakfast."

~ Lewis Carroll

8
Reality and Agreements...
Suturing the Heart

"If the new clan fails to 'see' you, do you really

cease to exist?"
— Metaphysical Quandary

"No one can change the path that you must go. The time will come around when you know that it's yours. Maybe there's a chance to go back ... home ... now that I have some directions." -The Wiz"

In 2007, I converted virtual reality into Real Time Manifestation. Once more I walked down the aisle
and pledged marital vows. As my family and friends stood on the sidelines witnessing my Whirlwind Romance, they had every right to be astonished.

At age 55, already a grandmother and at the point in life when people start to hang out the Resignation shingle, had dear sweet Becky Ruff gone off the deep end?

Yes, I had.

I threw myself into this new relationship as if I was love-and-sex-and-marriage starved. I was.

I was determined to prove to myself once and for all that it was possible to have a lasting lawful *romantic* relationship? I viewed this marriage as perhaps the last chance for some lust before the door slammed shut or any option at all dried up. I was free at last (I thought) to create that sacred bondage of fantasies with nothing and no one to stand in the way.

What I finally came to understand was that not only did I have the power to create whatever I liked, but also that *with the mere blink of an eye, my choices could alter my realities.* We design our life experiences in order to allow us to choose our outcomes. The greatest highs and lows are derived from those impetuous stirrings of the soul that are often referred to as "personal development."

*L*et it *B*egin!

As if I'd conjured my Gentleman from a wish list sent into

the ethers—POOF! He appeared… and like the overseer in

a Shakespearean play, I declared, "Let it begin!"

There I was, center stage in a typical TV drama top- loaded with crises, only mine were real and not resolved after 90 minutes as a "happily ever after" with ample time out for commercials.

I'd always had a fear of heights and now suddenly I found myself falling headlong into a field of dream-dust with a man I hardly knew yet who I was convinced filled every one of my desires.

Some formulas are made in heaven and others for rea- sons that remain unrevealed until activated. One of these is the Disaster Formula. Start with two extended families with different belief systems and
the normal amount of dysfunction (translate "plentiful with potential for more" when adding a new spouse to the mix).

In my case, from the male side, add a bipolar spouse with a bipolar step-son and demanding mother-in-law in a wheelchair with Attention Deficit Disorder.

From the female side, add my two lovely daughters, one of whom is a single mom experiencing post-partum depression, and two adorable grandbaby boys.

Then there's me, or the me I thought I was: age 55 and determined to squeeze my robust middle-aging mind- body into a Hollywood cross between Doris Day and Mary Poppins. Before this marriage started, I could confidently describe myself as smart, spunky and well-educated, with
lots of sunshine and common sense.

*My M*an

Let me pause here to brag about "*My Man*," delivered with the same emphasis as in the musical, *Porgy and Bess.* He is not only intelligent, charming and witty; he is also handsome and virile. Montana stock—strong in many ways, a jack of all trades, and kind. I go weak in the knees when he flashes his open smile, his ocean blue eyes shining with warmth and awareness—and a hint of a storm brewing.

Picture My Man in jeans and tee shirt with tussled hair when he removes his outside-work baseball cap. Not only is he smart; he also has integrity and compassion for others. And he's a good listener—for me, that's important. He lets me talk without turning me off.

I guess you'd say I'm a solid kind of gal, the type who's always willing to grab a hammer to help my male counterpart tackle household chores, work on vehicles and put up fencing.

To my great relief, photos of my man's past relation- ships and wives produced no competition whatsoever. In fact, they more-or-less resembled a photocopy of me: normal Wal-Mart shoppers or the invisible woman checking out your groceries, taking movie tickets, offering bakery samples at the supermarket, etc.

"Dreamy" is one typo away from "dreary." We started with the "m" version as we launched into that ideal courtship that I'd always craved. I felt valued, loved, even cherished, and didn't hesitate to reciprocate with my own contribution of joy and abundance. Both engines were running on hi-octane.

Unlike My Man's extended family, I had very little left; my parents had already passed away. They were living in the Southeast when my dad died and my mom, who died a couple of years ago, chose to remain in that area to be near my brother, his family and her extended family.

My mom was born on a farm and had joined the Marines during WWII. My dad was a corporate executive, also from the South. As his wife, my mom was the quint- essential corporate wife—articulate, charming and gracious.

Both were cultured, educated people who embraced the spiritual, holistic way of life. My father loved the English language and relished the power of both written and spoken word. My mother was a pianist who took syntax and mind expansion to the next level, applying its abstractions to her musical renditions; they were a good match.

Through the years as the obligations of their corporate lifestyle increased, they started to medicate their stress with alcohol. When my brother and I were in our teens, they decided to enter AA.

My parents' alcoholism must have demonstrated to me what I did not want in my life. I steered clear of substances, including all drugs with the exception of a few prescriptions.

The Sex Thing

My dad threw himself into his work and, to my mother's great disappointment, the passion that was left over was

delivered not to her but to his love for learning. My mother, like I, believed that an active sex life was the cornerstone of a happy marriage.

My mother never gave herself a chance to find the Holy Grail and now she's gone. That meant it was up to me to find it for both of us.

With my new Man, I seemed to be on The Trail at last. From the first day our friendship advanced to an intimacy and we started to explore the pleasure of each other, the sex was good. I was more than willing to overlook the rest… whatever that was going to look like.

So… What DID It Look Like?

Maybe it all started with a honeymoon that was over almost before it began. That weekend seemed to represent everything that continued to go wrong between the two of us.

Some people honeymoon for a couple weeks or at least a few days. Our post-wedding celebration was scheduled for a night and a day. That was it, and I didn't com- plain because I realized that My Man had gone to great trouble to rearrange almost

everything in his life to even get *that amount of tIme*

off from a new and

hectic work schedule and ongoing family demands.

He'd found a place where we wouldn't have to wait for the blood tests and I'd arranged for the hotel, license and minister. On the way to the blood place, my solar plexus started doing the butterfly thing... I was as nervous and skittish as an adolescent on her first date. All of this was so *romantic* and exciting! I was young again and here I

was with the Love of my Life, about to create that One and Only *Night to Remember!*

After a four-hour drive, we arrived at the hotel in time for a lovely dinner. By that time, My Man was already beat. He fell asleep soon after a picturesque walk on the lakeside where I'd managed to take a hard fall on the sand, ending up with a badly twisted knee and a lot of pain.

Was there a reason for this, I wondered, lying awake all night next to my soon-to-be husband, peacefully and deeply asleep. No sex and a painfully twisted body part?

The next morning we drove to the courthouse and parked by the lake where the minister met us for the ceremony. Directly afterward, we headed homeward. Tomorrow was a work day.

That was it, I kept repeating to myself. My
romantic honeymoon was over. I would still live at my own home,

two and a half hours away, for about a month.

This painful, loveless night landed at the top of my tally sheet. In place of butterflies was rage, remorse, regret—and disappointment. My Irish blood boiled over and I let loose. A "Ma chasing Pa with the fry pan" comic strip was nothing compared to Becky Ruff-now-Reed venting all her pent-up frustration on her dumbfounded groom (my evaluation, of course).

These tirades did not fall on deaf ears. For some reason he felt that both of us had probably explored the sexual arena so fully in previous relationships, it was

no longer necessary to give it much testosterone in this new one. This was evidenced by the fact that he'd thrown himself full-force into his new job. All that precious sex-energy was traveling to the office with him every day where he spent overlong hours and drove home in the wake of a trail of phone messages.

Is this the way it was going to be from now on? Maybe not, I told myself resolutely. Whenever I had a chance I continued to discuss with My Man my need for ROMANCE. *Hello... are you there? Earth to Moon? Can you understand my version of*

the English language?

Did he understand what I *really* needed, regardless of my age or number of times I'd walked down the aisle with others? I craved closeness, to be touched and held... to be told "I am the only one," etc., etc. I asked and kept asking,

and...

Finally I Got It

The first excursion of Togetherness and Private Time, "just the two of us," was a most exciting prospect. We both loved adventure and now we were going to combine that love with the other one and explore a wonderful new experience of fly-fishing. New for me but not for My Man.

He'd gone fly-fishing many times before, but this was a first for me. I was oh so eager to learn how to do it, especially since it was a sport that My Man, former partners, Mom & Sons had already enjoyed together. I longed for my own memory bank to add to theirs.

It must have been joyful for My Man to have a "buddy" to join him in the walk around the lake, I thought, my heart beating rapidly in anticipation

of what would inevitably follow.

The trek took us into a swampy mire. Obediently I followed, letting myself be led by My Man through muck and mud that was soon up to my thighs. On we trudged in the hot sun for about a quarter of a mile. By this time my arms, neck and head were covered with welts from hundreds, no *thousands* of mosquito bites.

Once more as on my honeymoon night when I'd twisted my knee, the tears came freely. Why couldn't this New Life be romantic and beautiful… and mud-and- mosquito-free, I sobbed.

*N*ext…

My Man understood, or so I thought. Next he told me he was going to take me river floating with inner-tubes, another first for me. Oh my, this did sound exciting and romantic!

Ahh, my outdoorsman! My Man was so skillful, so accomplished in areas where I'd had so little experience. To my credit were the *Indiana Jones and Temple of Doom* river crossings I'd done with my girls, but these paled compared to river floating with My Man.

Once we were in our tubes, however, instead of bliss I received a seemingly endless series of lectures about all the things I was doing wrong. My experienced husband tried to correct the way I paddled with my arms, the way I didn't always

catch the current with my feet pointing downstream; fussing at me for allowing myself to be caught in the directional flow of the current, and for failing to sit right in the tube.

I fought back my tears of frustration and hurt. Was this his idea of fun? "The concept of *fun* eludes you and your family, doesn't it?" I finally yelled out.

Never had I felt so much like an old horse that had already been put out to pasture. How could I ever ex- pect to be re-harnessed to a working team?! I was already up to my neck with all the lecturing and "not good enough" I'd received from both his mom and dad.

I hadn't yet recovered from all those mosquito bites and my bout with the mud, and here I was once again made

to feel "less than." *Enough!* I sobbed.

What made it even worse was the fact that I was already well-schooled from reading and listening to personal growth books and tapes that it was not *they* but *I* who was making myself into a victim.

I felt like I'd just pulled out the plug of joy from my own inner tube. Here I was going flat and drowning in self-pity, disgust and anger.

Actually, all of this wasn't far from the truth. My Man ended up about a mile down the river from me and before I knew what was happening, I found myself whipped around by the current and heading straight to- ward a fallen tree.

Without warning, the current yanked me under and into the

branches of the tree. My Man had told me to watch for that, hadn't he?!! As I became enmeshed in the branches, I had no choice except to let the tube go; instead of keeping me afloat, now it was pulling me under. With the current blasting my body, I struggled to get a foothold and felt myself growing cold and tired. Instead of wearing a tee shirt and cut-offs, foolishly I'd put on a swimsuit and now most of my body was cut, bruised and in pain.

By the time my husband reached me, I'd managed to become untangled from the tree, but I was so shaken and frightened, any notion of "fun" had vanished. That day I contributed many tears to the river. I was sore all over and feeling terribly sorry for myself. Yep, I'd got what I'd

asked for, I mourned.

A nd N ext...

Following this upset in the river, my mother-in-law started calling me several times a day to inquire when I might be well enough to take her and her wheelchair to her therapy sessions and various outings.

She thought I was a coupon from God.

Not only did I have money, I felt pressured to meet demands that had become almost unbearable. She assumed that her son's salary allowed free time for me to cater to her needs.

Can you hear the quiz show error button going off? Apparently she was unaware or it didn't seem to matter that I was supplying half the income for our union, as agreed upon prior to tying the knot. *Is this all I am to these people? An ATM machine and chauffeur?*

On the last excursion when I'd been transporting my mother-in-law to a beauty appointment, she decided she could guide me more easily once we were in the vehicle rather than giving me the street address in advance. During the entire drive, she made sure I understood that the shopping center where we were headed was on left side of the highway. As we approached the

area, she began shrieking, "Turn right! Turn right!" It's a good thing I'm fast on the brake and steering wheel and no cops were around.

Two days later I told my mother-in-law that I was planning an intimate evening with my husband because his work schedule had been so hectic. When that evening arrived, my mother-in-law sent her other 45-year-old son to our home to spend the night with us because we had a "better bed in the spare room."

There was no way to quietly say, "NO."

This woman was manipulating "my" new marriage, I sobbed. Notice the adjective, "my" when describing the union. I'd already expressed my anger earlier when my mother-in-law had attempted to have me befriend my husband's ex-wife, whom she adored, along with a few other friends who had "special" relationships with my husband.

Next mistake: In tears, I complained to my husband, who, like everyone else in the family, sided with his mother. After all, she was an invalid.

Was it Wrong to Want Privacy and Togetherness?

I've already introduced my new mother-in-law, at

least episodically. A strong matriarch who had convinced

her sons that her life had been filled with obstacles, she was demanding, strong-willed and judgmental (wasn't I all of these, too?).

She and her husband had owned and managed a restaurant/bar and they were also involved in other jointly owned family enterprises.

Now that she was confined to a wheelchair, occasionally

a walker and motorized cart, "Mom" routed her drives and energies into directing others. She felt that both of her grown sons and their spouses needed to reserve ample time in their lives to cater to her special needs. I didn't hesitate to voice my objections.

The physical injuries that had started on the night of our honeymoon "weekend" introduced me to continual day-to-day living with some level of pain. Every member of the family had been diagnosed with at least one disease or ailment that required medication.

Because of my own family's beliefs, transmitted to me at an early age, that something must be off-kilter for this type of physical pain to be occurring, I realized that I was witnessing a classic case of family dysfunction.

I felt so out of place and was so desperate to be accepted

as "one of the clan," I began to wonder if maybe I'd created my own set of injuries just to fit in. First the knee sprain followed closely by the accident with my entry level inner tube river floating experience...

Nope; joining the Meds Clan didn't do it either. I was still treated like an outsider. Added to this were "Mom's" tales of her expertise in fishing. She informed me that not only was she a sports enthusiast; she was also a successful entrepreneur and constant companion to her sons during the growing years.

How could I even begin to qualify as a buddy for My Man? I was such a *failure*...and that adjective of me was quietly and constantly enforced.

We were also forced to weather some financial crises precipitated from my spouse's generosity to previous

partners when he'd co-signed vehicle loans and trusted their tax preparations. Bank levies, over-optimistic purchases for the new house and legal emergencies with the alcoholic step-son added to the drama. My spouse said that he had anticipated that his income would provide a comfortable base, but often I found I had to not only match but often exceed his contribution.

B alancing A ct

Late night hours and relatives of this new family who were themselves struggling with life's upsets

sent me reeling. My step-son's aunt on his mother's side was the first piece of baggage dumped at our doorstep.

According to my new husband, "Susie" was "cute as a button." She did know how to push buttons, although I'm sure those were not the ones he was referring to. Susie, who was just going through a nasty divorce, had an ugly temper and habit of getting drunk almost daily. Our telephone answering machine overflowed with her "lascivious boy-toy stories" climaxing in seductive hints to my husband and finally, suicide threats. I called the local police, since that seemed like the "right" thing to do.

Apparently it was not; after all, Susie was overflowing

with the adorable gene and didn't need the police involved in her suicide attempts. My temper flared and I suddenly found myself becoming everything I found detestable in this woman and others who were button-cute

and/or manipulative and out of control.

Susie was the classic example of an abandoned woman and I was reflecting my own fear of being abandoned by my new husband. Whenever my temper flared, the simplest

look from my spouse would send my heart skittering. The unspoken script I was sending to my heart was "why did this man whom you so love *really* marry you?" I should have listened more closely.

Why was my new husband so forgiving of Susie's alcoholism? Possibly because he'd been on the same tread- mill himself during his early years. Did that allow him to enable his son "Todd," as well? I didn't think so, but I was not his father and "Todd" was not my child. However, I had begun to see a core of goodness in the young man which he rarely attempted to cultivate.

"Todd," who had chosen to medicate his bipolar dis- order with alcohol instead of prescription drugs, was a full-time maintenance project whenever he was home. In the evening when his father was at work—my husband worked long hours—my step-son would invite bar acquaintances to his burn pit in the front yard. It was difficult for me to set parameters, especially since I was still considered an outsider and deeply afraid of rejection.

My Family or No Family

My husband and his family members dominated our holiday gatherings with their traditions, and felt hurt when I wanted to alter these to encompass my small family's customs. His mom was used to my husband acting as a short order cook and staying in the kitchen.

My girls were used to having mom act as a banquet chef and hostess, making the rounds on holidays. "Todd" and

other family members took

over TV rights. My clan was accustomed to playing

music during the feast, with the men retiring to the den afterward for their football. Now there was only one channel choice for everyone: theirs.

Time seemed scarce for the two of us to be "just us" as we acclimated ourselves to our new life together. With my husband's grueling work schedule and round-the-clock calls from co-workers, I felt stifled and lost.

Lack of enough sleep. With as much strength as I could muster, I gathered all my inner forces to try to recover that lively, loving "me" that I honored and respected.

Attempting to explain my upsets to my spouse never ended well. The answer to my lack of cooperation or feelings of not being good enough was a standard: "Menopause is your problem. You are not being rational."

I don't do well with labels and categories. The generic catch-all statement "she's in menopause" brought up all the Irish in me, especially when it became a mantra for any type of divergent behavior I exhibited, including the expression of belief systems that differed from theirs.

Since I'm not yet "over the hill" and even if I were,

it would seem ludicrous to blame any type of disagreeable belief, thought, behavior and attitude on a woman's "menopause," the first comparison that comes to mind is telling an older gal she's "handsome"!! Or telling a short woman that she's "cute" or "perky" followed by, "It's okay to be short."

I realized that the authentic reason for my upsets occurred from feelings of estrangement. I thought perhaps my own insecurities made me feel this way.

I felt powerless to slow the spread of this chaos. My frustration, fear of what my life had become and feelings of being an outsider along with my growing financial worries made me feel like a screeching shrew and fish- wife gone mad.

My Irish temper roared. If I could distance myself I knew it would be raucously funny simply because all I needed to do was take a stand. Why was I so unwilling to do this? Why did I feel so committed to playing the role of victim?

I had been shown in so many ways that I wasn't what everyone in the family wanted. I knew I wasn't quite what my husband had expected. Just as important: I was an easy catch. I'd come to him with too much willingness.

I felt perhaps that I had wanted bliss so intently that just maybe I initiated the RAPID courtship. But that wasn't true. He and his mom had pushed that speedy wedding. And to my dismay, once the brief and highly unsatisfactory honeymoon was over, that was it. No romance, no great love relationship... just Life as Usual...I was expected to fill some role about which I remained uncertain.

What was I thinking? What was he thinking? His mom was quick to fill me in on My Man's romantic shortcomings that had apparently caused previous relationship breakages. I didn't understand why she would tell me.

He and I did not dialogue; we argued. In retrospect, I realized we had never really had a single in-depth conversation before getting married. I thought perhaps we were so busy with our own fantasies of "togetherness." But maybe I was rather extraneous to the whole deal. I was the supplier of funds and work-power.

I'm reminded of Michael Crichton's *Sphere* when I describe our communication challenges. "Earth to Moon, Moon to Earth: are you there?" We were like visiting explorers from vastly different planets.

"Of course we need time to mesh, honey," I'd smile sweetly at My Man after yet another blowup, "as long as we do it   NOW." But that was just my attempt at humor and accepting "responsibility" with my New Age ideas. I wanted to accept that I was only seeing my own viewpoint and that those of others were not totally self-centered. I surely didn't want to be a One Person Act. By this time, I had been told repeatedly that I was being selfish.

Directly before we were married, the first edition of *Romance Stew* was published. What amazing manifestation, I crowed after meeting My Man shortly on its heels. Talk about the Law of Attraction! In the book I had described my lengthy search for romance: connection with the right amount of testosterone to make it happen the way it does in Hollywood.

My husband said he'd read my book, and I was delighted to assume that he agreed with my perception of an ideal relationship, with the requirement of ROMANCE at the top of the list. At last, a man who understood and agreed with me about all the ingredients that were necessary   to create a delicious and nutritious "romance stew!"

I was ecstatic.

The Other Shoe

Soon after we were married, My Man admitted that he'd only read part of my book. The other shoe had just dropped.

I now realized more than ever before that our belief systems were radically different. He and the rest of his family did not believe that our thoughts create our beliefs, actions and deeds. Self-empowerment was a foreign concept.

My list of UN-acceptables continued to grow.

I continued to find rational excuses for the marital situation.

It was time for a therapist; we signed up for a joint

session during which we communicated with each other openly and honestly, or so I

BELIEVED.

We expressed that we both genuinely liked each other, and the only disparity came when the therapist suggested that my husband needed my help with his mother. She also correctly assessed that I was not keen to undertake a role of caregiver at this particular point in time.

Upon leaving the office, my husband and I recapped what we had learned about ourselves during the session. To my surprise, my husband "heard" that the lack of desire to assume the role of caregiver for his mom could be "fixed."

I felt I had been ambushed by his personal counselor. They talked over me most of the session – as if I weren't even there. They seemed to quietly make fun of my concerns.

What information had I not been given? Just what WAS the nature
of   THEIR   relationship?

"Nobody can make you feel inferior without your consent." - Elenor Roosevelt

9

AGREEING TO DIFFER

"WALK AWAY when something doesn't feel right, if you stay, you DESERVE what happens to you." - Family Heirloon

My Man and I had different ways of processing differences. I blew up and laid it all out on the table. Granted, this is often not attractive (!) nor does it rarely work when trying to communicate with a man who withdrew and clammed up.

I *wanted a verbal exchange* and couldn't get it with someone who refused to participate. Well, of course he refused! He found these debates to be total "no win" situations. Hs mother was in constant input mode. She was demanding as well as strongly opinioned. I was posturing as a saint and martyr. I was unwilling to accept that my new husband had spent most of his work life in the last

decades away from his parents. He now felt, it appeared, a great need to be close—not only to spend time, but to be available for them during the later years of their lives.

What was wrong with me? I was the one being expected to answer needs in his absence. The therapist had explained that I could not confront my spouse head on. She suggested that I ask for a time that was amenable to discuss concerns and upsets.

Of course this sounded reasonable. We never seemed to be able to find those spare moments for such discussions to occur. My husband worked long hours and was trailed home by a phone that never seemed to stop ringing. He told me he didn't have time for a wife.

I made my own bed, I kept saying to myself whenever I went into one of these rages. Things improved somewhat when the alcoholic step-son moved out of our home and into his girlfriend's apartment, but this was short-lived. I had never experienced life with a person who was a black hole of energy and whose drama had him taking over all of the life energy of those sharing his space—from his waking moments to his departure or sleep time. The drunken parties continued whenever Dad wasn't around.

Here's another thing that was getting to me:

My husband would tell me about all the younger women at work who were not only good-looking but also women of depth and integrity. Why would he do this to the woman he was supposed to love? It seemed to give him a glee in his own prowess.

"If I were younger and hadn't met you," he'd say, "I'd be at

(her) door as a suitor; she's quite something!"

Did he really have no idea how much those comments hurt me, and
when I expressed my upset to him rather than holding onto that feeling without saying anything—the feeling of being "less than," he seemed surprised. A friend suggested that it was his comfort with

me that allowed this freedom of expression. No, that wasn't it. I was out of my depth here because I realized my thoughts and feelings never entered his awareness. But people with whom I shared this wanted to assure me that it all seemed this way because of the newness of the marriage and the upsets so far. They were wrong.

Be Careful What You Ask For

A long time ago I'd actually placed a wish in the universe for a large and connected family. They would be gracious, loving and magnanimous, I dreamed, and they would accept each family member just as they were without trying to "fix" them.

The universe answered my wish, and added me to the list. Was I an accepting, non-judgmental, magnanimous, gracious and loving person, especially when "others" did not fold the towels the way I did, or make lasagna the only way their (own) children would eat it? This is what I wanted to believe. What actually developed was that I could never do anything that was

The Suturing Begins

I worked to put a New Age spin on things and brought my sense of humor out of mothballs. All my life beliefs urged me to color my present experience with their shadings of reality.

Maybe I was playing the martyr. Could that be it?

The heartache I was experiencing was like a cancer to my self-esteem.

A year had gone by since that dreadful honeymoon. At least now I could ask myself: "What am I choosing NOT to know consciously?"

And then... there it was! Right in broad daylight, just waiting for me to return from a visit with my daughters and grandsons; they are now living in my former house, a property I own. During the visit my daughters had suggested that I get my husband to agree to cutting the losses in the house he'd bought, but was our home. Then the two of us could return to my house and former lifestyle.

During the year of marriage, I'd gone through sixty thousand dollars of my savings, inheritance, and stocks to help My Man keep his dream—this house and this job— alive. They knew I was concerned about my financial state.

My Man had bought the house and the paperwork was finalized before he proposed to me. Before marriage while touring the new house, I met the former owner, a woman. My husband had already told me that he'd

placed her on his Wish List after meeting her on an internet match site (!). Upon meeting, however, this woman decided they weren't compatible. My husband had explained to me that she'd told him she preferred

big, muscular men. He certainly did not fit that description.

Half a year into our marriage, my husband and I were working outside and a visitor of the neighbors came over to chat for a bit. He let us know that he'd been engaged to the Wish List Former Home Owner, had lived with her and designed and created the upgrades and addition to the house.

I stared at the man and tried to recreate him as some- one who was "big and buff." Unfortunately, he could have been the twin of my spouse. My Man was visibly shaken.

Realizing his ego was bruised, we talked about it and to my surprise, he rationalized that the gal was experiencing the onset of MS (What happened to the menopause script, I wondered.) He said he felt she didn't want to impose her needs and those of her sons on him. He convinced himself (and wanted me to know this) that she'd taken the "high road" in rejecting his interest.

So much drama for my wee mind to absorb. Later I felt that he was only upset that he hadn't "won."

The other good part about all this was the fact that even though this Wish List Lady did not want a romantic liaison, she did have a piece of land with a lovely home to sell. Perfect! The housing marketing was already starting to slump and my husband's credit had been badly beaten up by

former wives. . . or so I was told.

The house was in an expensive area and needed much repair, but unquestionably it was a good buy. So, the agreement developed for the sale to be concluded in the contract for deed format.

I thought I was witnessing a man of power in manifesting.

Unhappiness for a new "wife in name only."

When I shared my sadness with my daughters—not understanding my own power of creation—lovingly they suggested I come "home" for a break. Driving the two and a half hours back to my spouse, I knew I could not go on pretending... but there was something that kept eluding me. Some data. What could I not permit myself to see?

My husband was glad to see me when I returned, and our conversation appeared to be going the same route. While visiting my family, I'd thrown out some possibilities to him like my returning to my house. He could then get roommates to meet his financial needs. Or he could let the house go back in the contract for deed and get an apartment in the city of his work, 50 miles away. However, I knew the house, land, and prestige of the location were of great importance to him.

I had to tell him that I simply could not make enough in any job to equal the portion of bill that had fallen to me.

One final option appeared to me and I shared this. He could return to his former job that required constant travel. The company would have been more than happy to take

him back and the pay was almost fifty percent more than what he was currently making.

I was part way into this exchange of real information and goals when impulsively I decided to go all the way. I asked my husband if he missed the kind of love he'd known with women where he ached… where these women took his breath away… where his heart sang and his very being

tingled.

I waited, holding my breath.

"No," he said. "Whenever I let my heart go like that in the past where I couldn't get enough of a love, it didn't work out, materially."

So there it was, lying like a flopping fish out of water. He'd never loved me as I'd wanted to be loved.

"OK," I sobbed in the bathtub.

But what else was I not seeing? There was something more…

I came out of the bath dripping water and tears and told my spouse that I loved him and that because I had wanted the love that he'd showered on his past partners, I'd thought his goodness and mine would bring it into fruition. Just like the scenes from the movies *Jerry Maguire* and *The Mirror Has Two Faces*, I also knew that I'd chosen to close my eyes and hope.

Existing in this strange neverland of high drama and the

constant tugs for me to accept their reality, I became trapped and WILLING in a dark energy hole of my very own creation which kept me sucked into an ever swirling quest for answers as to WHY nothing I did worked...and every practice I had been taught for success fell not only flat, but utterly failed.

I tried to bring my ideas of God back into my daily world. And my spouse and I continued for some months. I even imagined with a wishful state of avoidance that we were getting better.

In the *Thief in the Night* "Prophecy" saga, Gabrielle says to the young hero, "There is a plan, get used to it." This statement feels right to me because it supports my feeling that like a benevolent parent, God has a reason for giving us certain experiences, just as we have a reason for bringing these experiences into our lives. It's a two-way dialogue, not a one-way dictum. To this day I am still working on just what occurred.

Life and the universe really do have the answers. But the New Age ideas of accepting oneself did not apply as I kept plugging away, attempting to "make it so." I hid the results of being barraged by ever so slight acts and words of denigration about me and my family. Promises constantly broken, and my own identity evaporating to be anything required by his clan had deeply affected my inner core.

Will I ever have the romance I'm looking for? No...not with this partner and his clan of needs. I now realize that although change is always possible...and Love is truly a remarkable vibration of energy, the surreal life with someone - and in this case, many - possessing personality infractions of dysfunctional family links and narcissism, there are times when being used and discarded fails to fit happier New Age spheres. It takes courage to "see" what genuinely "is."

I watched a deeply disturbing Youtube presentation where a couple in a car had the women appear to go off the deep end, emotionally distraught. Reading about the episode, we discover that she was at the very end of her tether with her husband constantly breaking promises, manipulating her, using gas-lighting techniques, painful comparisons where one could never "measure up," along with that infamous style of "the silent treatment." This, too, had been my own experience. Health may be about accountability to self. Always "taking the high road" sounds oh-so responsible, but camouflaging reality can be dangerous to the heart...and soul. I remember that in the very beginning there were signs.

Coming into the union, I brought my wonderful old dog. I had waited too long to put her "to sleep" and on the final day, my spouse promised to help me get her 125 pound self to the veterinarian's.

As the day wore on, he failed to return my tearful calls ...Bless my old companion's heart...she hung on until she could no longer lift her head and I had to use a hand-truck, tape cardboard to it, and try to get her from he house to the car...funny in retrospect, but horribly sad at the time, I dropped her twice enroute to the car,

struggling to keep her on the dollie and to lift her into my car.

She loved me and looked at me with such compassion. Getting her to the vet's was such a heartbreaking trial...but she was ready to go.

My spouse was angry that I had continued to bother him...Just a sign of things to come.

My previous ideas remain accurate in a domain: Take
         responsibility for choices, have courage,
         keep faith, and remember the power of spirit
         that is you.

DEEP BREATH

Romance might be a paradox, but it should be more like the Broadway stage production of *On a Clear Day* by Lerner and Lane which delivers a joyful message of love and the inter-connection of everything in creation. Be wonderfully

free to follow your own path. And when the going gets tough or when fear sets in, know:

. . . There's more to us than surgeons can remove On a clear day, rise and look around you . . . and you'll see who you are. . . So much more were we born to do . . . should you Draw back the curtain, this I am certain You'll be impressed with you!

Don't be afraid and turn up the volume!

This simply is not the case with someone on the continuum of narcissism to psychopathy. there are alien styles of beings among us.

My reality morphs between living as a passionate warrior and that of a serene student of attunement. The idea is to flow with emotions and thoughts as circumstances change – and then to re-focus. Each of us has our own idea of thriving passionately. Life should become a game, with ethics as our individual hallmark.

What if the Real Truth is simply to find a merry-go- round horse, climb on and ride . . .Maybe that's what Dr. Courtney Brown, PhD. suggests with the idea of focus on energy threads of reality. It may not be "creating our world," but jumping lines of energy.

This chapter is the line of demarcation....As I look more closely at my choices and what I brought into my sphere, I have changed the font to note that I, too, have become vastly different from the me of the past...in a real way, I had to learn to release myself from the straight jacket of my own beliefs that left me vulnerable, inflexible, and unable to let go...

I find it particularly interesting in this era of our President Donald Trump that the effect of those on the narcissism to psychopathy continuum is so astoundingly far reaching. Whether the numbers of these presences are increasing or we are more aware, we have to pay attention.

Life in the Aftermath of a Psychopath & HIS CLAN

*The Meek Must Be Careful
Not to Inherit the Dirt...
(Ruth Joyce, my
mom)*

Taking the high road and expecting to
see goodness simply did not prepare
me for the fabulous acting skills of a
predator whose con game took more
than my energy and money...this being
and his clan struck at my soul...

No Longer Walking on Eggshells...

To all the women I've met
who share this experience
with me...
Amazing ladies (and men) – each and every
one...

" Relationships are like glass. Sometimes it's better to leave
them broken than try to hurt yourself putting it back together."
~Anonymous

10
THE LONE CAUSTIC COMEDIAN

What has been the greatest observation of myself as I look at my life with a narcissistic spouse and the bizarre hodgepodge of his family players who contributed to the warped dimension into which I had fallen? I must admit that this is all from my perspective. A dream I recently had comes to mind:

Sitting in the witness box next to the judge in a courtroom, the prosecutor poses two questions:

– Right after your spouse left you high and dry, following the evaporation of all your funds, hopes and dreams about the marriage,

and so easily moved on with another woman....

Would you – given a change of heart on his part - have tried one more time to make it work? **Yes, I *knew* the Hell (and thought I could make a difference for all....)**

AND

– Would you now? **No, I *knew* the Hell (and recognized there would be no difference for all...)**

This time of my life had been a trek through the bowels of the Twilight Zone. With all of the ups and downs of life, why had this particular journey been so devastatingly painful?

I believe the answer to be "betrayal." That is the seduction of a being using treachery. For me, it entailed taking the goodness within me – my choices, actions, and decisions to see the good in others – and twisting it, changing the "me" I had come to believe was stable and honorable. Turning my world upside down, I did indeed feel like Alice falling through the looking glass. My thoughts that I had grown and matured kept me on the path to what I believed was my ability to create the life I desired. However, agreements from others were necessary and that, as is said, was the rub.

Integrating feelings and choices in my life to that point, I felt there to be a purpose for connecting with others. My sense of closeness to my idea of God and the Universe was strong

AND

I not only sought, but eagerly awaited my older, feet-on-the-ground Prince Charming. When my spouse-to-be entered my scope of awareness, I felt seen and acknowledged. It was a heady kind of high. The show only gathered momentum when I met his invalid mother and her ailing spouse.

If emotions open a monologue with the soul, mine stood as a cryptically caustic comedian onstage. My heart so blatantly expressed its desire for that illusory and somehow unattainable entity of true love. Thinking, aha! this is it.

And just because it comes with some obstacles doesn't make this path any less alluring or sweet...I *belong*...I *am appreciated*...I *am needed for the unique attributes I bring along*. At this point in my life, I resemble a dark haired version of "Aunt Bea of The Andy Griffith Show" and finding a man who appeared calm, bright, communicative, AND had an excellent job seemed like Christmas!

However, coming into this particular production of "valued family and love" was like joining a circus... on a foreign planet. Or awaking from a coma to discover all that you held true for dealing with other people was amiss somehow. I remember episodes of science fiction shows where a person discovers one day that they no longer know the language, the rudimentary levels of letters and vocabulary.

Let me introduce you to some amazing authors who work to explain this land of smoke and mirrors.

Robert O'Connor, an amazing therapist, and Peter Shepherd of

www.trans4mind.com.

Betty LaLuna – (Facebook Blog – Narc Raider) your wheelbarrow- full of people and communication skills show you as a shining beacon of awareness and One of a Kind.

SAM VAKNIN whose work, **MalignantSelf-Love:Narcissism Revisited**, is the very cornerstone to understanding the narcissist and how he thinks, what his modus operandi is, how the patterns affect victims, what the confusion looks like, and the prognosis for both narcissist and survivor.

Thomas Sheridan for his **Puzzling People: The Labyrinth of the Psychopath**. Focusing on romantic relationships, Sheridan deals with the underbelly of psychopathy and explains the mental workings from the point of view of one who has a first hand account. He relates that many feel they have come in contact with an alien force. A total absence of empathy in the narcissist shocks those associated with the individual.

Although the narcissist has learned by social conditioning to observe and mimic emotions to fit into social structure, there usually exists continual drama and chaos in his realm.

WomenWhoLovePsychopaths
by Sandra L. Brown , MA

I was asked what kind of women attract the narcissist (and psychopath) - I just finished reading Sandra L. Brown, M.A.'s Women Who Love Psychopaths. This is an AMAZINGLY encompassing work and I'd say that coming through a relationship of inevitable harm, I found it relief-exploding in the evaluation of women who suffer from such contact. I said repeatedly that I felt my goodness was turned against me...and she categorizes just what and why this occurs....and "codependency" isn't in the mix. Women connected to the strange sycophant actually began the relationship "while impaired" - past periods of extended care-giving, loss such as divorce...even boredom. This is a unique study of the "victims" of psychopaths and their assets such as relationship investment. So many of the traits have been misdiagnosed as attachment formats.

This illustrates the predictable cycle of these relationships and why the bonding is so strong - how the woman, normally strong and vital, feels so fragile or mentally ill. Dissonance from the victim's perspective has a great deal to do with the psychopath's dichotomy of his childlike quality and adult mystique, not to mention communication skills and techniques.

The entire book is compiled with data, explanation, reason, and connectivity. There is no fluff within the covers.

The reasons we find ourselves captivated by these "alien essences" can be brought to light and Sandra Brown does this with clarity and an empathic comprehension - especially within the awareness of women because it is embarrassing being caught in the lure of sexuality. We are intelligent...and capable...and yet, we succumbed to some fairy tale - explained are the release of hormones and the staging by the psychopath, even the differentiation in his use of language.

We who have been taught that communication is the tool for problem solving, find ourselves in the

Twilight Zone. We are being held to incompatible standards.

There exist so many conflicts with belief systems, ideologies, and spiritual and religious principles where compassion is revered. It seems that we victims have been "hoisted on our own petards."

Ms. Brown's book covers everything I questioned....and it is an affirmation that "something wicked this way comes." I don't mean to sound so melodramatic that my review is discounted.

The AHA- moments were almost at every page, and most assuredly in every chapter. There is - if one enjoys science fiction - a correlation with the short-lived TV show, "Threshold." Awareness takes time.

I know many on blogs are "nutters" in their own right, mostly because they have not found the data to help themselves. So many therapists have simply not understood and the "pie-in-the-sky" New Thought folks have not come in contact with this form of "alien" presence. It's not that it is evil (maybe ?), but the two philosophies for life - those in healthy (just the ups and downs of routine dysfunctions, perhaps) states and those suffering psychopathy are simply incompatible. Your phrase, "relationships of inevitable harm" will forever ring true to me.

Here is the BIG QUESTION - and one ripe for a new book....because the numbers of psychopaths appear to be rising, how are we to live with these beings? I understand

the no contact rule and it is VITAL...but in the long run with the thought that these people cannot be treated, for humanity, what are we to do?

Every chapter in her book has dog-eared corners in my home. I carry it with me to the restroom, I return it to the coffee table...and I USE it for reference.

As always in this life, the lessons are much more about myself. AND Sandra's treatment of us victims is kind, observant, and chocked full of evaluational data. I am floored and delighted that there are explanations for super traits rather than that we have "failed" to be bright enough, wise enough, or even aware enough. I gleaned that my traits might just be valuable. Somewhere the patriarchal (and yet, I have learned that men can be victims, also)

Guidelines have become overly and overtly zealous. I don't believe it is as simplistic as relationships with authority that comes into question, although, our deep seated thoughts on "happily ever after" probably filters many of our personal scope of evaluations.

I am never quite as trusting as once I was...and because I have daughters and grandsons, I am alert to those in our realm and my own reactions to them. I'm not paranoid, but neither do I let a brief intuitive feeling flow past without a moment of appraisal.

I share my thoughts....so much is falling into place for me (and MANY others) because of THIS book, Women Who Love

Psychopaths, in particular. I have read Brown's other works, but this one is of monumental importance! There must be a more moving way to say this. It struck a chord of complete connection and affirmation within my very being and soul. There is REASON for the chaos into which I fell. And all with the best of intentions. It is not concisely ONE AHA-moment, but everything in the book.

The explanations cover daily life with a psychopath...the lure, the treatment, the forever changing terrain and MOST importantly the way we who fall prey respond. For me, this book relates to my daily heartaches, fears, anguish, and quest for my ideal. Not just of the relationship, but of the "me" I knew before this fear-fest of an encounter. The absolute torture was in the faltering grasp of my own humanity. AND to have AGREEMENT is CRUCIAL for survival...not just mouthed upsets and emotions, but to comprehend the why's. Interestingly, as I look over this review, I see the feelings expressed. Our society seems to be based on these very emotions and the need to join and establish rapport. Transferring our thoughts and feelings onto this "other" who is called a psychopath reminds me of Michael Crichton's book, Sphere. " What if the contact with an alien or artifact has no frame of reference for us as human beings" is the gist of the novel. It appears to have come to life today.

With profound respect and gratitude for allowing me to feel that my "style" of emotional sharing is NOT the CAUSE of the psychopath's evil in pinpointing me, I pass this book around.

It is, albeit, something to be watched and monitored by me, myself.

It's All About Him by Lisa E. Scott

In the midst of horrific anguish while freshly used, devalued, and discarded with the precision of a surgeon's scalpel in my marital relationship, I voraciously devoured reading material searching for answers to my trek through the bowels of the Twilight Zone. I was lost, alone, and terrified by the turn my life had taken, leaving me emotionally devastated and financially decimated. I stumbled onto a site with Lisa E. Scott's book, It's AlL About Him, and this became the turning point for my own self-redemption and healing. Lisa frees the confusion and offers a plausible and educated evaluation with the assignment of the term, narcissist. Ms. Scott shows herself to be a real woman of flesh and blood who struggled with her own angst in similar relationships and offers well researched data on narcissism peppered with stories of others falling into the dark abyss with this chameleon of a manipulator.

She takes you by the hand to allow each survivor reading her works a path of comprehension, knowledge that we are not alone, and the amazingly awe-inspiring feeling that we are not damaged goods who sought this painful excursion into an alien realm. Much more than this gift of hope and understanding are her accompanying blog sites filled with camaraderie and the deep and earnest desire to aid each other reclaim our self-esteem and lives.

Lisa E. Scott has another powerful book following the awareness of classification, The Path Forward. This manual clearly and effectively proposes essential steps for gradational movement into recovery.

Lisa becomes a valued confidante and friend in our individualized journeys to dropping the shackles of fear and self-doubt as we painstakingly incorporate mental and emotional purging and growth.

With intellect, warmth, and heartfelt compassion, Lisa has touched my being and essence. The courage to broach the topic of narcissism beyond simple defined traits and to sound the alarm that these disordered presences cannot be redeemed and must be avoided for one's sanity and productivity stands as her hallmark.

Her writings changed my perception of this dark territory and offered me a lifeline away from unaware therapists and unknowledgeable friends and family whose judgments left me drowning in uncertainty. Lisa brings herself, her generosity of being, and her indomitable spirit to "ride shotgun" as she coaches us to reach for aid, trust our instincts, and to live fully and consciously. She inspired me to write my own story. My life has been altered. I am no longer afraid and although not the same innocent I once was, I have the courage to stand for my convictions and to be fully myself, warts and all. Whether or not romance enters my future, I am OK and look toward tomorrows with fresh discernment and even an eagerness. There is nothing to hide and no attempts necessary to fit someone else's vision of me in a particular blueprint.

Lisa's works transformed my vision of being a desolate "sensitive" into one of personal strength and integrity, one step at a time. My gratitude is immeasurable.

"There may be times when we are powerless to prevent injustice, but there must never be a time when we fail to protest." --

Elie Wiesel

11

What my romance with "Mr. Right" Looked Like...

The Butterfly Effect has come to be recognized as a phrase indicating change. This altered path comes into being with the smallest of shifts occurring at an initial point. From that moment in a dynamic, non-linear system, not only does Robert Frost's poem take effect, but a swirl of reordering from apparent chaos develops.

"...I shall be telling this with a sigh
Somewhere ages and ages
hence: Two roads diverged in a
wood, and I-- I took the one less
traveled by,

And that has made all the difference."

For movie lovers, the scientist played by Jeff Goldblum in

"Jurassic Park" explains the theory of chaos to his traveling associate, a lady archaeological investigator . Dropping a small dash of water onto her hand a few times, he shows that the direction of flow cannot be predetermined because there exist too many minute factors and variables. Each time the droplet falls and reaches her hand, the path flows differently.

The instants of change for all of us as survivors come with a small alteration of our own beliefs – about ourselves, about others, about our experiences. Finding our lives ravaged by the raw pangs of our emotional states within the manipulations of a narcissist, we grasp for comprehension. Let me offer an excerpt from my own experiences to illustrate the total confusion and heartache.

My funds, almost $65,000, supplied the path to safety and he began to reinvest himself in his job and with his ailing parents. I pulled my side of the yolk with my mother-in-law who shared her diagnosis as a patient of possible Asperger's Syndrome. Her calls and demands for attention, social programming, and medical requirements increased exponentially. Being wheelchair bound and later unable to transfer herself, I was left solely to work with her and we spent hours at the ER, doctors' appointments, therapies, and exercising. Other family members only remembered this dominant personality as a wonderfully generous "mover and shaker" of independent strides in previous years and lacked any comprehension of the role into which I had fallen. Even saying this, there was love between us – or so it seemed.

As more responsibility fell to me with time spent in chemotherapy with his aged father and staying overnight at their home following rough episodes, the household hopefulness of new marriage expectation crumbled. I couldn't find my footing and appeared as an insane shrew. I cannot underscore enough my own mental and emotional upsets and the **havoc I wreaked on the home front**. My husband told me he had no time for a wife; he certainly didn't like me. He shared his feelings of infatuations about high ranking associates and his past online trysts.

> *My world careened out of control.* There was no romance – his adult son living with us became a link to redoing his past, it appeared. Connections to his son's mother jumped exponentially like some growing plague from "the Andromeda Strain." My spouse had no interest in sex or intimacy of any kind - just fatigue and an absence of desire to do anything solely with me. I worked as a hired hand on his property doing fencing, hauling heavy bags of cement, upgrades, and hosting family and functions - as well as footing the bill for a vast majority of activities, including chauffeuring his son with legal problems and no driver's license. In addition I put myself on the line writing on behalf of his son engulfed in criminal litigation. I was critiqued and criticized in never-ending loops of upset and drawing me back with promises of a great future. **Where had I dissolved?**

Persistence was my game plan as I believed in the concept of commitment in marriage...rational or not. Something had changed...

Continuing to wedge herself into some pseudo-wife slot by calling him at work, requesting groceries for him to drop by, and urging me to call him her assigned nicknames, it felt like she strove to make herself the dominant female – maybe the most important presence in everyone's life- perhaps part of Asperger's Syndrome as she had shared this diagnosis. She pushed to have me include her name on *gifts I gave to him. It was all too much and too close for my tastes.*

She called me on our first Christmas as a newlywed couple to demand I allow him to go away on a skiing trip with "the boys" to ease his stress from work and the marriage. She questioned me about our intimacies and wanted to bond over the lack of sex in both our marriages...she had a strikingly and uncomfortably odd interest in my spouse's sexual prowess. I sought answers and felt some ill fortune of emotional incest might be at play. This was like a terrible episode of the sitcom, "Everybody loves Raymond."

As I tumbled head over heels in free fall , I thought my honor required that I remain constantly participating in this marriage for Both my husband and myself. I searched for answers and surmised that the mother might be perpetrating emotional incest on my husband. Nothing in my large family background prepared me for this land at the bottom of "the rabbit hole." And there appeared no escape...at least while maintaining the union.

I worked as a contractor for many weeks at the small and growing company where my husband had supplied his devotion and received deep levels of appreciation and even adoration.

I found myself in the same inherent unpredictability that existed in my personal life, albeit, now with a break from his mother's to-do lists. There I watched in unexpected upset as the VP apparently sexually harassed a bright, attractive field supervisor. While attempting to carry on professionally – needing her job and trying to protect that of her significant other, also a supervisor – the distaste and confusion found itself written on her face daily. The old timers in the office turned a blind eye. I finally departed that post following several weeks without pay reaching contract personnel and services. It seemed insanity existed everywhere. Within six months, the company had cleared their debt to me.

My spouse's material "wishes" such as a boat, camper, motor home, and Harley Davidson found me floundering as an entity of any validity. Sadly, I quite simply did not say, "no."

I required knee surgery and the man I married stayed at the hospital during the procedure as his boss let him know that was expected. Returning home, he went to bed early leaving me alone to try to maneuver crutches to fill an ice-cooling machine for my knee. I felt deep hurt and abandonment.

His mother had let him know that this surgery was mild and required no extra care for me. After nursing him round the clock during many illnesses, a viral infection found me once. He was unable or in my mind, unwilling to help me. This underscored my place in the family unit and my flaccid condition as a being of worth – mostly in my own eyes.

In the throes of bankruptcy, he wasn't able to help me. Because my vanishing funds failed to answer his request

to rent a house down the road from his ailing parents, he moved our camper which we upgraded to a motor home onto his folks' property. Unwilling to share the bathroom and be at his mother's constant calls round-the- clock, I moved to my house two hours away. My funds were to have allowed me to aid my daughter with a career while I made a small income by watching her sons, one with severe health problems. My spouse had become an important member of my little clan and the grandsons, ages 3 and 4, loved him. And then, there were all the promises of "tomorrows" with hopeful expectation. Looking back, I was horribly naive. The mothers sister and brother and the ex-wife of a son thought of her as a saint. Was I missing something? Was I not understanding a larger family? I was surely out-of-sync with my spouse's sense of responsibility and loyalty to his family.

I continued to visit almost every weekend where I was his mom's caregiver, shopper, provider of housework and lawn care as well as helping the father. It was painful to watch what I felt was the dysfunctional relationship between my spouse and his father showing traits of a perfectionist. Once I helped the dad wash and hang curtains and we had to measure every pleat for exactness and every point along the rod - the drain on energy was amazing. In my time with them, nothing my spouse did was ever correct enough *and this very fact tied me more strongly to "be there" for him.* With failed marriages under my

belt, I honestly believed I could "love it into being." My rules of operation may well have been mine alone.

I acknowledged that the strain on my spouse was immense, giving exorbitant amounts of "positive energy" to him in my attempts to put my belief systems into play. He withdrew and took a vacation with his first wife, visiting his adult sons. I was shaken and wounded and acted as if I were mentally unbalanced. She remained always a peripheral player in the picture of his life. Other women, I discovered, had taken their leave of what I called this insane asylum and vanished, avoiding all contact. Now, with my knowledge and awareness, I can understand this "no contact" rule. Back in this period of my life, I was shipwrecked and stranded out of my depth. Some "female" health concerns reached my state of consciousness and I had myself tested for venereal disease. Fortunately, I had none. Not until much later did I discover the evidence of many online romances by my spouse. Re-connections with Facebook "once-upon-a-timers."

The daughters of long ago passions seemed to trigger a sense of grandiosity in my partner. I was drowning in a sea of disbelief and utter devastation. The lifeline of my old belief systems simply couldn't keep up with each new episode of upset and my responses. The strength of mind and spirit I felt to be part of my essence crumbled.

The voice-mail he left was bitter toward me for failing him. The litany of unpleasantness he had experienced in previous relationships, he managed to replicate with me within the first year of our marriage, almost as a cleansing process. Still believing the idea of working through problems to keep the marriage alive, I plead with him to talk to me and go to counseling. He agreed - with his therapist, not the wisest choice, but the only way the session could occur. I broached the topic of covert incest being perpetrated by the mother. The conference seemed to go smoothly and additional times were scheduled. His therapist assured me that he "was a good man and wanted to be a good provider." Apparently his use of silent treatments was considered acceptable as she reminded me that I couldn't have disagreements with him "head on"....I would have to first get his agreement for a time and place appropriate. Unfortunately, with his 24/7 job and his parents' needs, there was no acceptable time allocation. I was to go along with the agenda. I was being an aid to him by taking on so much within the relationship and handling the burden of his mother, and his therapist wanted me to remember this.

What in the world was wrong with this picture? Why did I stand for this in my life? **WHERE was I?**

That one session was the end of counseling. He immediately canceled the additional time slots with no word to me. Calling the therapist to verify the next contact, she coldly relayed via her receptionist that he was her client alone. I felt confused and once again out-of-focus. I can't say that I would have viewed myself any differently with the data coming from him. I felt like the song lyrics from "The Sound of Music" where describing the nuns' feelings of being out-of-focus with the whirl of their young charge's energies and chaos.

There had been such reaching and withdrawal from him along the path of our troubled marriage coupled with
threats of divorce whenever I was unable to acquiesce to some material desire.

Whenever his much appreciated manager had relationship difficulties, our life also fell into that pattern, as if to mirror the company's style. Our last reconciliation had occurred just a month prior to this.. He had

joyfully made plans for a vacation with me, upgrading my washing machine at the house because I had given my new one to his mother, and creating a solarium with hot tub. The constant sense of being off balance surfaced again.

I finally allowed my brain to process that my money was the

primary interest to him. On our last time together, the reality of my financial state and absence of any stash of funds registered with him. Within two weeks he had planned a future with another gal and was winging his way in some high adventure. It was over. I had declined to be a caregiver for his mom. When the step-father died just following our last visit, my spouse's out-of-town brothers and their wives came for the "dance of mourners" and played their roles to the hilt. His new lady-fair was rallied into the "clan." I was expunged...erased...It was as though I had never existed.

All the nights I spent with the aged and declining father, following bad spells in chemotherapy, transporting him to medical appointments and staying with him at the nursing staff's requests, hours talking with him and helping him in his garage simply faded. The three days per week for a year and a half that I gave to the invalid, wheelchair bound mother to be her care provider, housekeeper, yard work aid, errand runner, and supplier of additional funds for groceries and prescriptions...the repayment of my spouse's loans to the couple...all began to vanish in thoughts and memories as if the timekeepers in Stephen King's "Langoliers"had come to life.

The entire grouping of family members needed to reboot their existences and show a united front. They seemed to have decided to reinvent the family, its members, the histories shared and put an entirely new spin on the mother's reality and that of my spouse's choices, irresponsibility, flagrant abuse of me, and present emotional standing.

There would be no goodbyes. There would be no closure. There would – for some time – be no sense of understanding and no reason behind the production so much like John Carpenter's horror story, "In the Mouth of Madness." I, too, had interacted and added exquisite twists on my unbelievably and unearthly all-too-real nightmare.

No wonder his therapist felt I might have attachment disorder. I was never privy to the content of their sessions. She remained keenly connected to his privacy and I, in the dark about his version of the story line being fed to her, existed in an exquisitely detached purgatory. I was receiving the reach-and-withdraw scenario and silent treatments for days on end. Then, the grand shows of renewed affection along with gusto at a continued union. Never, however, an apology. No wonder the diagnosis of codependency falls all-so-often into the mix. For lack of the professional terminology, "I was SCREWED UP."

After just three short years, I was a morphed version of myself...and not at all "better."

"Half the harm that is done in this world Is due to people who want to feel important.

They don't mean to do harm — but the harm does not interest them.

Or they do not see it, or they justify it Because they are absorbed in the endless struggle To think well of themselves."

~T.S. Elliott

12
LEFT ON MY OWN

My first thoughts after I found myself so unceremoniously discarded were to find someone else who might ease the pain of this thwarted romance. I really knew that finding any kind of suitable male partner with whom to consummate a togetherness would alleviate the angst – for awhile, but only for a brief moment in time. At that stage I just hoped to somehow squelch the deep sadness. I did, however, recognize that I needed time to simply be myself, be by myself, and to trust that the woman I'd discover would be worthwhile. Fortunately, the Fates put no interested parties in my path...I would have to go this agony - and pretty much by myself. I found some blogs which allowed the leeway to groan and express all the hidden fears. My family members were loving – in spite of being worn out by the maddening roller coaster of emotions I exhibited in this relationship and my apparent lunacy in forcefully determining to make a go of the marriage – in spite of reality camping on my door step.

My search to comprehend the drastic changes in my life's direction AND my place in the scheme of things had me reading anything viably close to what I had experienced. I read voraciously. I stumbled upon the concept of narcissism and this defined "essence" so clearly mimicked my own personal ride into the previously unknown to me stretches of Hades.

Sandra L. Brown and her book, How to Spot a Dangerous Man Before You Get Involved, *led me to her site: saferelationships.com. Was I in a pathological relationship?_*

Something about my introduction to the idea of narcissism struck a chord. A personal look at the disorder and its consequences were open to view at narcissism101.com. Even the TV personality Dr. Drew has been talking about this.

A definition that I found excellent is the pattern of traits and behaviors which involve obsession with one's self to the exclusion of the awareness of others and how they are affected. It involves a ruthless pursuit of ambition, dominance, and gratification (wordig.com/definition/narcissism. The two markers that I could so readily agree with are the fragile ego and self-esteem and the lack of empathy. These traits are severe and yet the individual can present so very well. In his chameleon-like life, my partner was adept at reading situations – most of the time – and was facile in his ability to change.

One of the most diabolical tags to pin on the recipient of a narcissist's energies is the word, codependent.

I find myself at odds with that immediately. This seems to be a very old school approach to evaluating the "victim." With the labeling of the recipient of the narcissist's litany of upset and his reach and withdrawal techniques, we contribute to allowing the narcissist to slide in the area of accountability. My now ex-spouse's female therapist held him in high regard.

Because I fought to keep the marriage, she tossed the idea that I might have attachment disorder. Our use of her as a marriage counselor – even for one time – was not in the best interest of the marriage. I truly was at a disadvantage. I had no idea that he had wanted out and told her so. The professed love and desire to create a life together, through all life's bumps had me working overtime to make a go of this – never realizing it was all a show. Being a viable and special partner to him was not a permanent slot for me. I had always felt a lack of gusto in the intimacy department, but the excuses of a new job and stress made sense. I wanted to be kind and appreciative. Being sensitive in an empathic way more reasonably describes those of us who have not only fallen prey, but who have been sought by the self-ordained "one." Sympathy requires more of a down-scale attitude. In sympathy,there exists a parallel of susceptibility of life's experiences. Whereas, sensitivity seems inclusive while valuing the other individual. It would appear that the narcissist is trying valiantly to be well rounded in his life position.

Those offering sympathy shower another with attitudes of "you poor dear." But the narcissist apparently comprehends this system of balancing the scales to be too heavily stacked on the one side. He seems to strive to encompass a more well situated person to complete himself. In this sense, it's not at all like the "Jerry Maguire" idea of a love partner "completing his counterpart." The feel of the vanishing strengthening-associate is more along the lines of the victim of a sycophant. Unfortunately, instead of living symbiotically, the narcissist seeks to prove that he is enough by himself alone.

The results to the sensitive are more invasive than just denigrating that being; they include the attempt to erase her presence once the need has been served. The paradox in narcissism would be the need to form a strong, safe unit while proving anything beyond himself remains extraneous and unnecessary.

So, why do we who are the sensitive in the relationship struggle with such angst? Perhaps we catch a glimpse of a formidable quality of greatness that might exist - if any of the acting had the slightest basis of truthful emotion. The associate was sought and even courted during that grand phase of "being in love" only to be *un-chosen* once the emotional vampire became OK for a while. To need a romantic alliance on the one hand, only to hate that poverty in conscious feeling on the other must be a living nightmare for the one existing within the bubble of egomania. But, perhaps that is attributing too much within humanity's description to this creature.

The narcissist uses the doctrine that individual self-interest is the valid end of all actions. In egotism, there exists a sense of exaggerated self importance. And there is a difference in the context of being self absorbed. With egoism, the accountability philosophy falls away.

"Every day you either see a scar or courage. Where you dwell will define your struggle."

~ Dodinsky

13
Camelot's Round Table

Against all reason, the heartache of being so unceremoniously duped and dumped clung to me like some invisible straight jacket. Sandra L. Brown talks about the "inevitable harm" from any relationship which MUST follow in one with a psychopath. I always felt my goodness had been twisted and turned against me...and the greatest anguish of heightened pain in excruciating manner came with my knowledge that I had allowed this to happen to me. The tentacles of a deranged state of mind had interwoven themselves among my own beliefs, honorable intentions, and connection to life itself. This was a science-fiction play moving into this plane of existence. Fear became my daily companion. Had I EVER existed?

Yes...the answer is YES. There are so many kind souls who did not judge me. Robert O'Connor, a therapist is one among many.

Another is the bankruptcy attorney, who couldn't help me as an individual, but surely exuded kindness in his role as trustee handling my spouse's indebtedness. Somewhere and somehow as my life was unraveling, I gathered the gumption in time to file as a creditor in my

spouse's bankruptcy proceedings. Some divine intervention shook me by the shoulders because at this intersection of the story, I was rattled, dazed, unbelievably confused...AND STILL feeling it would all work out...somehow. I tried to discover what I could have done differently.

The Powers That Be gently forced my hand. By this time, I had experienced an astounding and alarmingly fearful crisis of faith. There were those who wanted to label me and find some horrific flaws in my past that could explain it all, permitting this participation in events to be categorized and filed safely away from a need to deal with the repercussions. It was like being on the out-of-water end of the quickly sinking Titanic. There was no escape. I didn't ask "why has God allowed this," but "is there EVEN a god?" Had all my beliefs and high flying New Thought, upbeat wisdom ever existed as valuable and worthwhile forces of energy? I was more terrified than I had ever been in my 58 years.

When giving birth to my daughters, I had life and death situations due to complications, but then I had my faith and belief systems on which to hold fast. Now, there was a blank slate and nothing to ease the learning process. The overriding awareness was that this "trek through the bowels of the Twilight Zone" had been REAL. It was still "real." Distance away from the rigors of "the clan" and the man I believe o be a narcissist did not eliminate the daily hum of thoughts about them, how and why I had evaluated as I did, who I was, and what I was now to do. The expanse of separation DID allow me to release my endless quest to ask the never ending loop of questions of others. I had in my darker moments plucked strangers from grocery store lines to share my tale and pray that they might offer some morsel of understanding which could form an infinitesimal nugget of truth on which to build.

During this "dark night of the soul," I stumbled upon books and blog sites. I discovered I was not alone in this sea of putrid reality. There were others writing and distributing ideas along with their own narratives. This wasn't "home" in the sense that one could rest and rejuvenate. It was, however, a safety net to grab. And I hung on.

Such guilt surfaced. I had failed devastatingly. My hopes and dreams, and romantic images had been quashed. My material wealth, inheritance, retirement, and lifetime of savings had evaporated, always with the promise of having time to regroup. I had failed my daughters and grandchildren. My plans to supply funds for the purchase of homes, trips to expand their horizons, money to make their lives just a little easier – all were drained and awash because there incontrovertibly would be no way to recoup.

I have needed to let that culpability and self-reproach slide into the past. My focus will be in survival now.

Let's remember what we have discovered in our journey into no- man's land...Science doesn't support the concept that this is ONLY a psychological disorder of personality divergence from mainstream population. Perhaps it might be true of some labeled as a narcissist, but there is also something terribly destructive in another segment labeled with "narcissistic personality disorder." It presents the overwhelming prospect of incontrovertible harm to any who have met the new, detrimentally "improved" war machine of the NPD.

They are bright, adaptable, quite cunning in their manipulative

skills and prepared to do whatever is necessary to make themselves feel better and look more acceptable, often turning the tables on the victim. We now can detail and expose just what the victim finds her life to become - AND WHY. The super-glue attraction (and no, it's NOT codependency), trance-like suggestibility, disintegration of the victim causing her to feel she can't leave....and the total absence of remorse on the part of the perpetrator all form the backdrops to life with these individuals. We use the phrase, "lack of empathy," almost cavalierly. It is as if dealing with an alien species that has NO concept of our values, belief systems, and communication expectations toward safety in sharing.

The existence of a benign version of the "beast" may be present, HOWEVER, that should be relabeled. For any who have been completely blindsided and treated as the feast for the attacking vampire-entity, it has resulted in "INEVITABLE HARM" (S. Brown) on so many levels to the victim. We must not think that the narcissist carries a lesser evil in his/her pursuit of well being.

It/he/she does not improve by thinking it so. There will be no alteration that makes this being comprehensible. This condition is becoming pandemic AND it is changing the definition of humanity and our society's structure.

However, there is now a beginning awareness. There exist so many of us out there in the world at large. "Something wicked *really* this way comes." As time has dulled the offensive agony of the torture to my own soul and sense of being-ness, I find there remains much for which to be grateful. The consciousness of benefits in this life has begun to fill my heart once more. It's a start. I had wanted to make a difference.

"You can gain more friends by being yourself than you can by putting up a front. You can gain more friends by building people up than you can by tearing them down. And you can gain more friends by taking a few minutes from each day to do something kind for someone, whether it be a friend or a complete stranger. What a difference one person can make!"~ Sasha Azevedo

My last tango of a marriage and its drawing down the curtain on the last act of that particular play has left me quieter, but finally, not unhappy.

My brother, 2 ½ years my junior, has always been a man of honor and integrity. We found ourselves in a decade long estrangement due some to our mom and much to his now ex-wife.

Communication which was always huge in our lives, took a "time out" in that period. With mom's last days approaching, we broached any real and imagined differences and took steps toward reclaiming the strong bonds of love and loyalty that had engulfed us in our early lives together.

He and his present wife represent my hopes and dreams of envisioned rationale in the "life together with commitment" scenario. I want them to have joy and bliss and travel this highway of love and laughter...with just enough challenge to make the trip breath-taking and inspiring. I want the very same possibilities for my two daughters in their own lives.

At 59, I suspect I've taken down my "romance at all costs" shingle from my front doorway. But, I'll look in on it and shine it from time to time. I did seek that elusive "Camelot" of high adventure with its invention of fanciful sentiment.

Although I did encounter and even initiate heroically marvelous deeds in the quest for my evasive dream, the lighthearted zest more than occasionally found itself dashed by life's details and unexpectedness.

AND with all the exasperation, it truly was worth the passage.

So, now, with a limited arsenal of skills, I can share my story with you. You can survive. I have. YOU have so much more to offer this world than the years of confusion made you think. Reach out to many...take a step....search for rekindled visions and inspired emotions.

Always be thankful for the gifts in this lifetime, no matter what difficulties may also come along. So many of us will be here for you. Remember falling on the playground, bloodying your knees? It never occurred to you not to get up. That's still inside you – and each of us. We are a bit like a bag of M&M's...many colors and all uniquely whole...We might be a little melted, but we're still here.

"God made Truth with many doors to welcome every believer who knocks on them." ~ Kahlil Gibran

However, that grabber emotion – the same intensity which caught us each in a trap with the narcissist/psychopath – was mandated to close the circuit and ignite truth...infuse courage...and liberate valor.

Betty LaLuna spoke with emotion and aggressively refreshing realization that we, the survivors, must acknowledge it all – our choices, the heartbreak, the essence of being targeted, and the connection to each other as we all - both men and women, worked through the out-of- focus sense of ruptured time and belief that had come to us in this strangely lit continuum. She brought her velocity of spirit to the written page on Facebook and our new-found awareness took flight.

Within her musings all of us victims/survivors discovered unabashed beauty, human fallibility, and wisdom. We had forgotten that we each had a spark of Divine light within us; we had been so beaten down and almost mortally wounded. This is the legacy of Betty LaLuna. It is easy to sense and feel her heart, soul, and even the anguish of her own journey. The utter SPUNK that kept her moving forward, pushed me to continue plugging away....She is REAL...her life has been no fairy tale. This camaraderie grew from much more than comparable aspects of this state where knowledge was gained.

We all had our developing stories through direct observation and participation. The corresponding evolutions of all of us were the road map for directions out of Hades. All of us who are survivors exist on a path of our own inner domains...and yes, demons. And, yet, we are not alone – much due to the animating principles of life offered so freely on the blog.

In some instances certain members on blog sites railed against others through frustration, pain, and fear. As a moderator of style and moral-discipline, Ms. LaLuna rose above judgment and held a steady course for all of us to follow. At a time in my life when my heart cried in agony,

despair, and total confusion, she spoke to me, and so many others, with her candor and the reality of constant renewal in living every day - putting food on the table in the midst of personal upheaval, handling responsibilities, shoring the dikes of everyday living, and putting one foot in front of the other. Betty LaLuna gave us hope...made us laugh, allowed us to cry, and offered a hand to climb out of the swamp of disbelief to begin to climb into our own NEWLY refurbished reality.

With irreverence, wit, and unflappable grace, she reminds each of us to be the best of which we are capable under such trying circumstances and with the information at hand. Our factual information, reasoning, and ability to process after being shattered increases constantly and we are prodded by the heart of the blog and its members to continue – sometimes in inches, and once-in-a-while in leaps. We have accepted that forgiveness is part of the path, but it is indeed a long course of proceedings. To relinquish a sense of requital exists separately from burying one's head in the sand with the hope it might all simply go quietly into the night The desolation found by so many victims must be recognized and validated.

The crux of successful blog sites is to raise its member to the realm of warriors of truth and decency. As Sandra L. Brown so clearly explains, we who have survived carried super traits that when mixed with the pathological presence formed a highly volatile and quite toxic "cocktail of attraction." Those essences of hyper-connectivity, high relationship investment, skyrocket levels of compassion, and the willingness to take risks have a place in our world, but most assuredly NOT with a psychopath. Finally, relinquishing the fear of our own choices that led to the mess of our present lives, we can stand on our own two feet and see not only who we are but of what we are truly capable.

We survivors need not hide, being afraid our own foibles will be seen.

We stand as a bucket brigade, offering a hand to the next one in line. The time has come to question the old forms of information. This land of pathological influence must give way to our indivisible whole selves and our Don Quixote image. **The meek must be careful not to inherit the dirt.**

"Today's Rainbow : The Rabbit Hole Really IS the Tree of
Knowledge
*When the Mist of life with a Narcissist
Evaporates"* ~
Me

14
A MASTER'S DEGREE PROGRAM

Love doesn't always bring the curtain down on a happily-ever-after theme. Even so, I sought enough good times to offer balance with life's rough patches. Meeting "my particular" narcissist proved such a disconcerting trek into unknown territory. Loving and losing as I have described in my journey's discourse was to be a learning experience beyond any I could have fashioned in my wildest fantasies.

With a spouse I feel to be a narcissist/psychopath, it felt like a Master's Degree program on shifting sands.

I had participated in acquiring practical knowledge in the arena of romance and relationships. Now, at 58, I can admit that I have been a tool for learning for others as well as being affected by the nuances of this search for connectedness within love myself. With age and some maturity under my belt, I felt myself to be   realistic.

With my new spouse, I held such joyful expectation – in the beginning.

I was fully aware of changes and altered choices along the sometimes rocky path to romance. This is such an example – where narcissism was not the chief player. In my once playful look at romance and finding that wonderful partner with whom to grow old, I had both joys and sorrows – all within normal parameters of dating and wandering through the halls of relationships.

I find myself much in agreement with the scientist/physicist, Nassim Haramein. Perhaps creating this reality of 3-D existence isn't quite as the New Age folks suggest. It involves more than putting out vibrations of what you wish to manifest. There is a cycle of activity wherein we are affected by others and our created world is also affected by others, as we contribute to the wholeness of their masterpieces. In my story of romance that didn't quite reach that fairy tale summit, I learned a great deal about love and the ability to give without requiring a specified outcome.

> "Reaching" is a wonder. It's dramatic and exciting...and occasionally a bit heavily spiced with drama. In looking at loving others, we are also discovering how to love ourselves.

"Man has gone long enough, or even too long, without being man enough to face the simple truth that the trouble with man is man."

~James Thurber

Hope does indeed spring eternal! The closer I move toward antiquity, the more knowledgeable I become about me.

Surely, that must promise the successful outcome of AN

appropriate union – one of appreciation, respect, physical intimacy, responsibility, and lots of laughter! A quote from Bix Bender comes to mind, "a gate only works if a corral comes with it." Let's make our own corrals worth opening the gate.

I wonder if passion can really exist with a person who feels solely in line with Destiny. There is a marvelous story by Henry James, "The Beast in the Jungle." John Marcher is forever expecting some monumentally notable fate to befall him. May Bertram becomes his friend and confidante, offering an amazing depth of compassion and companionship. Marcher sees her as an adjunct to his life and never fully recognizes her uniqueness or connection to him, the man.

Suffering ill health, she makes a striking plea for him to accept her love for him as she shakily stands at their last meeting before life's flow leaves her. He is incapable of understanding the gesture and continues along his mental route of titillating watchfulness for that moment when destiny meets him. Excessive pride and self- involvement kept real life at bay with

Archer. Always seeking that illusive unspecified thing in his future had him forfeit passion – of any kind. And that was Fate's amazing "something" that pounced upon his awareness at the end of his search. He had allowed absolutely nothing of passionate depth into his existence.

Being a romantic, I look back over my marriage to the narcissistic spouse and can see so much of John Marcher in him. In our case, I would have striven to continue. Perhaps by coldly removing my tether ropes to him, he sought yet again to find that perfectly flawless connection and relationship. I cannot help but wonder if he forever tried to remake his history with his mother where this time there would be not only accolades for him as her son, but that she might applaud him as a

distinctly unique and separate force of presence. Instead, mental illness and a mighty fortress of pharmaceuticals held the post of his medicine cabinets.

I can remember our first night together as man and wife in our own home. He came in from work and was Angry that dinner was not waiting...even though he had told me that he always wished to shower and change Before the meal. and baffled me. The level of his upset hurt.

Soon after that promise of never going to bed angry evaporated. It seemed I forever failed to satisfy the to-do list such as moving a huge mound of dirt by shovel and wheelbarrow to the side from the front of the house. In my free time from working for his mom as a personal care provider and ATM, I was to cut the weeds in the lot behind his house....get fencing ready....clean the garage...paint the house...and simply be "quiet" like some piece of furniture.

"I've put in so many enigmas and puzzles that it will keep the professors busy for centuries arguing over what I meant, and that's the only way of insuring one's immortality." ~James Joyce

15
BELIEVE

I have to admit that a sense of humor – either during or sometime after events – kept my life moving forward many times, one step at a time. I could easily be the quintessential poster child for failed romances and the last one with a narcissist surely took me into the realm of eerily uncanny expeditions to the dark side. I believe that I understand something of the phenomenon of New Thinking as shown by Eckhart Tolle and his premise (as with so many others in this particular path of thought) that there is only the Now. Because living entails an emotional response, that "Now" is a point in time where we not only observe ourselves in dramas and settings, but where we feel the emotional flows of energy emanating from our views in that scenario.

Anyone who exists within time frames also looks at the future, responsibility, cause and effect, choices of the past, and the precipitate of fallout from any specific action taken in response

to a stimulus of some sort. But, what I have come to see for myself is that our emotional responses to "something" will not alter the occurrence...it does, however, make being in that present time more acceptable or frightening/upsetting, depending on the point of introspection.

With utter despair and excruciating distress, I discovered myself discarded by a spouse and his family when my funds had run dry and anything I offered of myself produced no useful end for them. I began searching desperately to find a way to cope with MY NOW. The pain of loss was almost unbearable – much more so than any other relationship breakup in my personal experience. I feel that my discovery of the term with its ideas, narcissism, answered my driving need to label this phenomenon. As a lay person, my search bares my stamp.

In the midst of horrific anguish while freshly used, devalued, and discarded with the precision of a surgeon's scalpel in my marital relationship, I voraciously devoured reading material searching for answers to my trek through the bowels of the Twilight Zone. I was lost, alone, and terrified by the turn my life had taken, leaving me emotionally devastated and financially decimated.

There is a path of comprehension that I needed to find. Just as in the movie, "I, Robot," where we discover that even these beings of other-than-flesh-and-blood presence tend to group together when stored away from activity, I, too, needed to *know* that I wasn't alone. What I sought was some kind of understanding of what had occurred, a sense of camaraderie to counteract the responses of friends and family, and most importantly, the amazingly awe-inspiring feeling that we –

specifically, me - might not be damaged goods who sought this painful excursion into an alien realm. Sam Vaknin, himself, has been diagnosed as a psychopath and still his books and videos are exceptionally informative.

The "sensitive" as coined by Scott, which I so much prefer to "codependent," strives to fathom the uncharted experience when compared to past relationships and teachings about communication offering an avenue for connection.

Eventually - and the time frame for healing may continue for two or so years – each of us rummaging through our beliefs following this excursion into total confusion, will change her/his personal vision of desolation into one of strength, integrity, and the ability to reclaim one's life.

I detested the idea that seemed to predominate within the ranks of therapists that codependency was *only* bad and indicative of my own deep rooted "illness." In a period of my life when just emerging from continual chaos and turmoil, this itself, seemed like a conspiracy to eradicate any validation of my own experiences. It seemed much too simplistic in fostering the idea that low self-esteem was the problem in all instances, to be "cured" in the victim. Even if the intentions of counselors were good, they certainly created sustained roadblocks for a willingness to communicate freely for fear of being chastised with labels. This, indeed, was my own movie played in the midst of a strangely entangled family. What I found tremendously distasteful was the thought that my response to a genuinely horrific experience was pathological itself.

Through reading books and joining blog sites, I found it to be true that I had begun to effectively climb a course of purposely essential steps of gradational movement into recovery. It's a most individualized journey to dropping the shackles of fear and self- doubt as I painstakingly incorporated mental and emotional purging and growth. Being tested in a very unique way, I, too, have found my own nodding acquaintance with intellect, warmth, and heartfelt compassion.

I discovered that I needed to change my perceptions and ideas on past teachings regarding other people and even the hallmarks of communication. My track of development included rethinking my own conduct in this dark territory and with some difficulty, offered me a lifeline away from unaware therapists and knowledgeable friends and family whose judgments left me drowning in uncertainty. Learning to trust my choices and again to live consciously has been a most enlightening procedure.

There is repetition of much of the material and efforting in these chapters because that is THE process of digesting, regurgitating, and operating on a new awareness that may well go against every lesson from religious teachings.

My life has been altered. I am finally no longer afraid and although not the same innocent I once was, I have the courage to stand for my convictions and to be fully myself, warts and all. Whether or not romance enters my future, I am OK and look toward tomorrows with fresh discernment and even an eagerness. There is nothing to hide and no attempts necessary to fit the vision of someone else for me in a particular blueprint. I have now transformed my vision of myself as being a desolate "sensitive" into one of personal strength and integrity, one step at a time. My gratitude to energies in this universe and all who shared their testimonials with me is immeasurable.

Perhaps in seeking a romantic dream state, I've discovered just how magnificent humanity can be. We strive for goodness, on the whole. We find ourselves bloodied and bowed, and yet we rise to face another day. It's an adventure ...a trek of self-exploration.

"...what is there in a storm that moves me so ?
Why am I so much better and stronger and more
certain of life when a storm is passing ? I do not
know, and yet I love a storm more,
            far more, than anything in
nature." (Kahlil Gibran's letter
August 14, 1912)

16
Nebulous Concept

What I sensed for some time and was not able to
formulate into a clear idea is that this phenomenon is not
Just a psychological disorder on the part of the perpetrator.
There is some essence that **differs GREATLY from the
rest of us.** The narcissist in this recent life experience of
mine deviates fantastically from other personages on
whom the labeling trait of "narcissist" has been placed. As I
look back , being a year and a half out of the ordeal in my
marriage with the strangely unfeeling spouse, invalid
mother-in- law, and overwhelmingly present also-bipolar

adult stepson, I see that "unfeeling" is simply not the correct adjective or description of the encounter. It truly is foreign.   It   is   pathological. Let me share my thoughts on this. There exists a more precient awareness of the changing direction of our society and culture today with the introduction of writings on relationship narcissism from Lisa E.Scott's *It's All About Him,* Sandra Brown's *How to Spot and Dangerous Man,* and Sam Vaknin's *Malignant Self Love.*   To include the emotional impact of such encounters and resulting "dark night of the soul," for recipients of this psychological act, blog sites must be included such as

that of Betty LaLuna and her Narc Raider on Facebook. Something insidious has altered life perspective across the world regarding a sense of detachment with no empathy.

Public social networking has brought a surprising focus to this imposing occurrence. Howard Bloom writes of change in comprehensive thinking and actions that lead to the survival of societies in his book, Global Brain, and these impressively thought provoking encounters in the literary field strive to calmly elucidate developments.

Narcissism appears to be rapidly gaining the high ground within a growing number in our populations who simply fail to comprehend the well being of others, as if those being encountered unaffectedly cease to exist once the viewer's attention passes. This takes the phenomenon of New Thinking's "living in the now" as expressed by Eckhart Tolle into a totally alien realm.

What may be a first stage in an altered path for society can be seen within the relationship abuses where one of the couple presents as a narcissist – not in narcissistic traits that we all possess, but in an adversely foreign approach to connecting with others. Thomas Sheridan, a bit off the beaten path as an author with his thoughts on reptilian brain programming within man, also writes clearly about this behavioral event in his book, Puzzling People.

Posters to amazingly numerous blog sites share experiences of striking similarity with personal results in horrific anguish for the relationship partner, changing her or his ability to cope with life and most definitely sinking these individuals into realms of dark confusion, following periods of chaos with the narcissist. Although some within the halls of therapy dismiss this state by attributing the pain to the catch-all category of codependency, Scott refers to those easily used, devalued, and discarded as "sensitives." The "trek through the bowels of the twilight zone" reaches well beyond emotional devastation to include financially decimating the recipient of the narcissist's actions and expunging her sense of defined self to encompass even the loss of trust in basic belief systems.

Brainwashing develops through techniques of gas lighting, withholding communication, and sheer contradictions by removing the "victim" from the company of those with whom shared thought and emotions exist. The attempt to amend ideology works toward "social influence" by changing behavior, attitudes, and beliefs. The alarming note should sound with the apparent pandemic of this behavioral alteration which also presents in the corporate realm, workplace environment, and bullying in schools. Our culture is morphing in ways that redefine humanity.

What sparks a surprised note of amazement is the commonality of the utter anguish described by the "victims" of a narcissistic relationship. These women AND men come from different life scenarios...different educational realms...and with different backgrounds. No simplistic patterns of abuse can be shown before the events with this perpetrator.

A psychologist checking my idea suggested I look at the type of person that would be attracted to a real narcissist My first thought was that I was going to be pigeon-holed as a pathetic being. I had a not-so-grand encounter with my ex's therapist.

> I disagree strongly with so many therapists who lump all into the easy category of codependency. For myself, I felt totally alone - left to wade through the muck by unaware therapists, family without knowledge, and friends who couldn't for their very souls evaluate WHY I didn't hang it up and call it a day...in my case, my track record was one of cutting the cord when things just failed to work into a reasonable facsimile of what I deemed a healthy relationship. And that may in itself prove a strong clue - I thought I had acquired enough wisdom, experience, and strong base of belief systems that I just might weather the negatives to pass into a thriving and long-term relationship.

> Not all who find themselves in this predicament are needy and suffering the dregs of low self-esteem.

> Granted, I surely was *within* the ordeal. I think it is an open person of courage and integrity who might keep plugging away. There is always

risk in putting ones toes into the lake of relationships....the strings and connections find links beyond the partner, alone...I don't think it's a curse, at all. Connection forms society.

Integrity comes into play because we acknowledge the best in others...albeit going with the idea that this very "choice" of seeing PERCEIVED goodness will shuttle in it's coming to pass....is rather ludicrous, at best. However, it's a doctrine in our social beliefs. One I had felt valid.

I also put a lot of stock in my ex's therapist who told me I was helping him when he dropped his demanding invalid mother with Asperger's Syndrome into my daily routines. And when I attended a couple of joint sessions, with her guiding him, the two had such a great rapport that I felt like an eavesdropping outsider as they talked over me ..and about me in the third person. Now *THAT'S* something to look at a bit more closely. Was it some essence of ME that initiated this cavalier approach

to my pain?

I'd like to share a funny remembrance. The therapist and my now ex-spouse laughed about my keeping a clean kitchen and washing dishes rather than letting them sit. If I had been asked, I would have responded that THAT was where I could have some sense of control in all the unending chaos and dramas that came with my spouse and his clan. The "family" dramas, trials, and tribulations flourished in their domain. No one genuinely wanted answers or resolutions. They seemed to seek a type of grand-standing in which others might evaluate them as "good" and worthy of sympathy. New Thinking folks that I had respected and with whom I even shared a synchronicity of thoughts kept telling me that I "created" my life. So, by the proposition, "if a equals x and x is greater than b"....what was wrong with me?

I used to believe and say that, too...now, I feel more that I do have choice, but a great deal exists in how one responds to some unfathomable situations that materialize from other fields and people involved.

Looking at Athens and Sparta, examples used in Howard Bloom's book, it was almost classically male/female....and the "female" side was consumed by the more aggressive Sparta - BUT the valuable traits of Athens in her culture and enlightenment survived. In my marriage, I wasn't to be absorbed, but actually erased after my purpose was served, leaving no trace or memory of me.

I have changed...there is an innocence that is missing...not a naiveté, but the almost too natural   trust I had in others has

drifted. **I have also changed with the turmoil of a period of loss of faith. It was a dark place in which to find myself. Not "why has God forsaken me," but "IS**

there even a god?" "Is this just a PRISON planet?" The foundations of my belief systems were truly shaken.....I think more from having my ideas of "goodness" turned against me. THAT could be real codependency.

I will share that the publisher I once used could see and validate her authors who wrote of strange excursions away from the norm, but chastised me for showing myself to be "so passive." I think that is probably the crux. When one is willing to let something unfold with time and the idea is present that a better development can be found if enough patience and use of relationship building blocks can be mustered; this can be seen as (that funny phrase comes to mind) "too stupid to live." But, with me, hope truly did "spring eternal." My spouse and I were – apparently – such a fantastic match in the beginning...communication was in open sharing and our goals operated in tandem. Reason said we could find that common ground, again. That is all part of the complicated staging process. To an outsider looking at this unfolding drama, there is no sense to be made of the charade.

Charade and masks find imminent importance for the acting of someone donning the title of a narcissist. I'm not at all sure that most of the psychologically disordered aren't actually psychopaths. Labeling at the lower end of the spectrum gives a sense that this anguish-filled experience wasn't detrimental to the spirit and heart of the survivor. It was.

The definitive signs of psychopathy are an encompassing pattern of disregard for others, for the rights of others, and include a lack of empathy and remorse. There are false emotions involved and the ability to fit into social standards with manipulative tendencies.

Grandiosity and deceptiveness play strongly. The disordered personality can be impulsive, irritable, prone to a lack of accountability and even aggression. There exists a predominant inability to perceive danger. The actor provides an amazing performance of acceptability in many cases

and actually learns to adapt his style for his own needs. The victim may provide a meal ticket, funds, a place to live, sex, or standing in the social order. Once the needs have been filled, the victim or target is often devalued, denigrated, and discarded without a second backward glance.

These presences are very frequently described as "alien" because they do not operate with compassion. Our problem in society is that we are preconditioned to use kindness and responsibility and are slow to accept that the disordered person may actually behave without any guidelines that we might comprehend.

As I sorted my timeline, I wrote a fable:

Armageddon Came Stealthily
"Freedom is the right to tell people what they do not want to hear."
~George Orwell

Once upon a time in a land called Earth, a species known as hominid developed and populated the great globe.

Surviving travail and cultural crises, the societies rumbled forward – many individuals and groups striving for the betterment of mankind. There did occur apparent deviations from global empathy, but the other sectors of mankind continued to right their vector momentum and crusade toward higher goals of mass survival and opportunity to thrive as both individuals and congregations. The criteria focused upon uplifted values and ethical perspectives for both mankind and the Earth.

As the citizenry grew, New Thought in the molding of ideas acted as a placebo in calming and guiding the more highly educated and industrialized beings. With the study of this domain of knowledge, presences could choose thought patterns and people with whom to associate. This path carried them away from the hubbub of troubles and daily engrossment in procuring the needs for base physical continuation and those of remedially soothing influences on emotional drives.

Preoccupied with attainment of beliefs and systems of convictions of truth, and with confidence in this habit of mind, the inhabitants with all the privileges of free men became less aware of other activities in their realm. The great institutions of learning had categorized knowledge, functionality, reasoning, and had even established schools of remediation for aberrant intent of cogitation.

Within this finely tuned paradigm developed a tumor-like deviation of being whose thought processes did not house the ability to experience empathy. The vast scholarly institutions held that this was a psychological impulse of will, could be corrected, and went about the business of formulating treatments to reestablish balance for the individual, and thus, society as a whole.

Insurgency began to arise within small numbers of natives who disagreed with those within the great halls of understanding and their comprehension of truth. Straying from the hallmarks of data and using primitive observation, these rebels began to formulate a new idea – one divergent from the psychological treatment vectors. This new concept began to take shape as those within society reported horrific anguish from contact with a differing strain of hominid. In these encounters, individuals found themselves mesmerized, deprived of their original self-hood, callously used, devalued while following the best and highest forms of their belief systems, having their values and purposes shaken, and then unceremoniously "left for dead." Rarely could aid be found to salve the damaged psyches of the victims, for the true believers of the old psychology formats simply were unable to fit the data into their stable and well-acknowledged schools of belief.

Could it be that this uncustomary encounter with a divergent strain of citizen could be more than a mutual tangency with an abnormally motivated being? What if an influential drive was not the root, but an intrinsic style of operation? How were the majority of presences to relate to this, and more to the point, how were they to protect themselves from emotional harm? These relationships proved unavoidably destructive to the well-being of individuals and filtered to society.

The insurgents pooled efforts, information, and unified contact to discover an amazing similarity with experiential reports. The strange behaviors of a group of beings whose common description could be a total absence of empathy began to form the base of understanding an event-horizon for any who remained in contact. The most honored notions of forgiveness could not hold stasis and a return to valued normality with this uncharted manner of conduct.

To remain viably humane and uphold the values of their domain, the primary citizens recognized that the exclusion of "the others" was not an option and yet, there might be no rehabilitation possible for this new strain of presence. They would need to define a new application of learning which might offer tools to formally acknowledge actions coupled with intuitive feelings of those coming in contact with the alien co-citizenry. In addition, techniques would be required to heal the damaged persons left in the wake of such predators.

The glorious past eras of golden virtues might have faded, but a fearless approach to handling the challenge of meshing two entirely foreign ideologies for joint survival on the globe called Earth would stand as a gateway. This ascension would bring change to the tried and true beliefs of the departed generations and perhaps a tarnished overview of life as that given by the prophets and teachers of great creeds. Today would prove an opening to a road of awareness. Knowledge, itself, is not power, but the ability to use that information and to do so with righteous intent would mark an evolving humanity as it strives to incorporate the incompatible into a new world. We, the insurgents are not the same. And so, it begins......

It is important to acknowledge my own traits and needs that drew me into this sphere of experience and even repeated performances within my past.

"To explore what it would mean to live fully, sensually alive and passionately on purpose, I have to drop my preconceived ideas of who and what I am." ~ Dawna Markova

17

Soap Opera Revisited

During this period of my life when I evolved from being OK with me and seeking a romantic partner, to the time of working with the aftermath of life with someone I believe to be a narcissist – after finding a not-so-Mr. Right, my youngest adult daughter used her humor to suggest a book title for follow up – (In Relationships when One says: On, no...it's not you, it's me...) Guess What? It Really IS YOU! I have to admit that tickles me. My life's trainings had been to accept responsibility for my own choices and to be accountable. This particular trek past purgatory and down through Hades genuinely sent me reeling. My ideas of constancy and focus of attention on the union, putting one step in front of the other proved part of some false prophecy or play in which I was the only involved character who had no clue about the director's aim. To this day I still feel blindsided by being so used, devalued, and discarded with not a backward glance from my narcissistic spouse and his clan.

The key operating attitude existed within the entire group of his family unit. My oldest daughter, an appreciator of anthropology, believes that it can take long periods of time to effectively change the route of a society's thinking patterns. The culture media of developing individuals forces a shift in drives for survival and this affects each segment of the whole. However, there may also exist physiological hiccups within mental processes of the lone actor.

I can recall being so saddened by the stepfather's death and with the out-of-area sons and their wives arriving, along with my now "ex" and his girlfriend, it was as if I had never existed...times over the three years with the ailing parents were erased in the blink of an eye. My relatives hated what happened with this group of people and with that, I had no way to grieve for the loss of the older man, whom I had come to love. It was an excellent reminder that life is in "the now." My "now" was elsewhere. Grief for the stepfather and the memories of our times together and shared ideas and conversations would have to be totally my own. This proved a rough but beneficial healing mechanism for me. Whatever exists across the barrier of space and time...and death, I could now choose *my memories* and *the emotions attached to them,* after finally "seeing this tribe of takers" and recognizing that reality. I won't pretend it's not a process to let go of hurts.

The scenario pretty much existed that I had been "left for dead." This would certainly have been a mighty bitter pill if it were all in the emotional realm, but it also hit my economic life, leaving me to start from ground zero with no funds. The most awful feeling was that I could no longer offer any really substantial aid to my children and their families as had been my intention. There would be no rescue and I am in the process of working through the devastation. I had envisioned something quite different for my 58th year of life.

Here's the very basic truth for me. I had set my parameters of this life in my faith and positive thinking. The uplifting self-help ezines such as Peter Shepherd's "Cultivate Life" were a bit too lofty at this juncture. It wasn't that I didn't wish to reclaim my beliefs of old; it was that they did not fit my present suit of experience. Hubbard from Scientology would have surmised that I had dropped down- scale and would need to climb

through emotional tones to rise toward happiness, productivity, and serenity. I knew and presently know there is much truth in many upbeat good works.

Unfortunately, I felt as if I had been ousted from a college fraternity or sorority of the "beliefs realm." Life and even reason had taken a shift, leaving me to grasp at hazy ideas.

Looking at articles from the magazine, Psychology Today, I admit to being perplexed by the changes within the standards of "correct thinking." I can remember books and articles about doing the work one loves and having the money follow. Now, some of the lettered elite Ph.D.'s cite sources stating that making money by doing what you love can decrease creativity. Continuity of beliefs has shown itself to be of major importance to my sense of stability and it seemed to be lacking wherever I turned.

I understand my late mom's thinking as being on shaky ground in her last days. She had weathered her own relationship upheavals and surprises and had remained strong, vital, and autonomous. My brother lived close to her and finally had to push her to rescind her driver's license. It was to her a sign of independence and she gave it up, fighting all the way. But, having mown down all her neighbor's hedges when backing out of her short driveway, there simply was no more leeway in sheer yardage to offer freedom for maneuvering.

Perspective is both amazing *and* frightening, especially when a decision must be made.

Twenty-some years younger than mom when she passed, I can definitely relate to her feelings of dread in losing this signpost of liberty.

And, of course, it was painful for my brother. Shortly after this milestone, mom's health began to deteriorate quite rapidly. My brother being a marvelous man, moved his wife and himself along with mom back from his house into her home to allow her the dignity to "call many of her own shots"...the final stages of her life were unwinding. Her ideas of independence and wishing never to pose a burden to her children faltered with the realities of physical needs. A relatively short period passed before mom finally said adieu.

My sense of self was shaken in my last marital excursion, just as discernibly as mom's in in her coming to grips with a turn in her life's plans. I took my best ideas and dreams into the realm and at times became a raving lunatic. I really had won the lead in "The Taming of the Shrew" without the delightful ending. I look back over the drama's frame of three years to see a woman (me) overworked as a hired hand and construction aid, personal care attendant, chauffeur, maid, errand girl, mediator, bookkeeper and household manager to see myself within a troubled – or at least, Alternately-dubbed – marriage.

There was little joy and an overflow of demands on me to

produce for his entire family. I permitted such abuse. I thought I was part of the group and family and had made a commitment. There were oh-so embarrassing moments when I not only desperately longed for warmth from my spouse, but after layers of exhaustion had been reached with a man withholding intimate and sexual contact, playing reach and withdraw games with the silent treatment, I could not comprehend how our premarital decisions about openness and respect disappeared. Looking at myself from the outside, I really did appear absolutely crazy...or at the very least as a manipulative and pouting teen.

There were nights I followed him into the bedroom and I screamed, shrieked at him – trying to get a response. We had discussed so many ideas and concepts about marriage before the legal commitment. One of the greatest methodologies of "how to survive Arguments" was never to go to bed angry.

Like so many other choices that I had felt we had agreed upon, this seemed of no importance to him. He often went to bed by 8:30 at night, just after dinner. There was no alone time as a couple and with his adult son living with us, his comfort about intimacy was even less that before. Well, that was the reasoning. Just recently I watched an episode of "Everybody Loves Raymond" where the main character's shrew of a mom does much the same to her husband who is feeling dejected and ignores her, completely. It's not pretty, but desperation in trying to use old techniques to establish communication comes at such a cost. There is great humor in the sitcom, but it's awfully close to home.

So, the old ideas and philosophies have needed to undergo re-evaluation. This has absolutely nothing to do with one's feelings being hurt. All the re-creating of one's life deals with re-establishing the boundaries of self. Ultimately it isn't therapists, family, friends, or pets who give us purpose and meaning. We have to find that within ourselves. And when we – certainly I - so recklessly offer outlandish trial and error methods, I definitely had to rethink my chosen convictions. Who in the world was "doing the thinking" behind the me doing the thinking? Did my belief systems work for me? Not in this arena. Before a brush with narcissism, these had been more than adequate, but now, I had seen something ugly in this activity of animate existence.

Therefore, thinking "It Really IS you!" has great appeal! In my personal sphere, all this transpired as I was undergoing menopause.

Although the once rampaging hormones ceased to dance, I remember musing from time to time that I liked being a female. Can you hear the tune and lyrics from "The Flower Drum Song" musical, "I Enjoy Being a Girl"? I'd like to feel a bit of that zest again.

My Own Reflection

"Belief in oneself is one of the most important bricks in building any successful venture." ~ Lydia Child

Looking back, I was still strong enough to sense that I was responsible for my own survival...and it had to be now. Even through the early part of our separation, I thought there might be a return to our initial stage of marriage. However, looking back into that time, his mother's demands had yanked me right out of the starting gate. His family's needs to handle financial crises, host and pay for family functions, offer a safe haven for the adult, troubled step-son, and be available for personal care to both his parents – the invalid mother and her husband's chemotherapy regimen demanded attention and I was all so ready to step up to the plate. This was the life I had chosen and a commitment had been made.

Recognizing that I had been duped and now had to pick up the pieces, I put one foot in front of the other and mustered the tattered remnants of gumption to put my claim in his bankruptcy case together. I had no funds and could not locate an attorney who'd work with me without a hefty retainer. My thoughts were still dazed, and I could not and just would not believe that I had been exploited so startlingly and with absolute strategic precision. My emotional devastation was real and heartrending. Eat, work, sleep as best I could, and *remember to breathe.* I was still me. But I was dazed and sorely wounded.

I couldn't even smile at the thought that I so looked like that sad and frightened deer, caught and catatonic within the glare of the vehicle's headlights. My movements were mechanical and the dreams and racing panic-filled thoughts tumbled in my mind. Never before had I been so unprepared, disorganized, and ill equipped to move forward.

That last Christmas together occurred because he cajoled me into his visiting and playing the role of stepfather and grandfather. He lived on his parents' property in our camper and came to my home sporadically. I had in my saner moments begun looking at financial avenues to allow me to sever ties. With the decision to remain available to his ailing parents during his bankruptcy, he had told his mom that he would spend time with me, his wife, much over her constant to-do lists and desiring him to be at their beck and call even on weekends. This constant offering of tidbits to satisfy me had me teetering in a state of indecision. By that December I was worn out and needed some space from all the family dramas and asked him to stay at his folks. He played quite the role of desiring to be a viable member of the family on my side of the state.

We shared a most unusually personal and sensual holiday season where he told me that was the way it should be between us. We renewed our shared love of Kahlil Gibran under the subdued romantic lights in the living room at night. My heart thought, ah....we are going to make it. Work and his parents kept him away until Easter where he arrived again to share a lovely holiday with my daughters and grandsons. He made plans for our upcoming anniversary and vacation. He seemed sad to leave. Within two weeks I received a voice-mail telling me that he was going forward with a divorce. During our years of marriage, that would be the card he played when attempting to have his way, usually involving money. That Easter he brought photos of land he wanted to buy "for us" – I was surprised because of the bankruptcy proceedings underway. Finally I underscored how unfeasible this path would be: it dawned on me that he expected me to pay for it...he hadn't believed that all my funds had disappeared helping him and his family in their never ending black hold of crises and needs. By his departure he accepted that my savings, retirement, and inheritance were gone.

It seems that he had rekindled a "great" love from the past and they had been planning for her to move her family into his mother's home. To be fair to his next "love," she had been told that he had been separated for years – and the charade was not unveiled by his clan.   She had a nest egg.

As pictures of his adventures with his new love and her children found their way to my Facebook page, I finally accepted that I existed within that clan no longer. He was content to make no legal changes for awhile as he watched and evaluated, but I pushed him to file for a divorce. I was now almost financially destitute and needed help from the State to keep my physical form alive and going.

My personal funds or lack of those required that I file pro se and with a fee waiver. I contacted legal aid which could only make a couple of quick suggestions. The responses and my created "exhibits" of paperwork were intelligible and comprehensible...somehow. One year from that Christmas turning point found us both "unwed." His work demands had decreased, his mother lived elsewhere, and his adult son lived out-of-state. He had a clean slate economically and could play the grand provider and head of a new household. What had my positive belief systems done for me in all of this?

They actually saved me from deep bitterness. As my recovery from the horrific four years trudged from day to day, I grew better able to cope with this change of direction. I wrote bits and pieces of articles which proved therapeutic as I deconstructed the past events. Choice. I always had choice. Naiveté. There was that, too. I had been a simpleton, so longing for the fairy tale romance. More like Grimm's Fairy tales in their dark humor. I had been the Aunt Bea character to his Don Juan and was totally swept away by my ideas of fairy tales and positive thinking.

At the approach of the first anniversary of my divorce, snatches of pain, although dull, once in a while touch my awareness. But these are reflective...without attachment...
and I am me once again. I'm alive and I've survived.

My tiny house is home to amazingly independent pets. All with unique and unmistakable personalities. Money still proves something of a struggle, but the personal anguish of it all has faded. I am grateful. I find myself more often wrapped in an agreeable appreciation of kindness and the simple actions of daily life. The return of faith happened in the passing of days with quiet entry once more into the me that I felt had faded. This "she" is returning. However, it would take almost a decade for the full fleshing out of me to return.

My easy-answers in my New Age days no longer come from that place. I feel we each must earnestly choose to "see" and handle the fall-out.

"Our life is a faint tracing on the surface of mystery, like the idle, curved tunnels of leaf miners on the surface of a leaf. We must somehow take a wider view, look at the whole landscape, really see it, and describe what's going on here. Then we can at least wail the right question into the swaddling band of darkness, or, if it comes to that, choir the proper praise."

~Annie Dillard

18

Background Connectedness

My younger brother and I were always close in our youth. Time surviving the heartaches of life with violent alcoholic parents had forged quite a bond. Our parents joined AA in the last steps of our high school years and life improved, allowing us to return from foster care. When my father died, I was living with an aunt and uncle, attending college. My brother had his own memories with the differences of treatment in father/daughter and mother/son relationships. Comparing memories, we'd laugh at the disparities and how we would view these, from the outside, as if they came from two different families.

Our adult years found us raising families – I had more than one marriage and his of 31 years came to a wrenching halt when his wife met someone online and left him behind. There is much love, compassion, and camaraderie between us. His now ex-wife forced a rift between us that lasted almost a decade, but this chasm healed near mom's death.

So, comes the wonderful little phrase that we use – It is what it is...and what it is, is.

A very dearly beloved friend of my brother's had a quirky sense of humor. Personally, I thought he might be operating a few bricks shy of a full load, but his huge heart took up any slack. He used that expression whenever developments in life happened beyond his scope of comprehension. Through the decades, my brother and I have turned to that delightfully funny phrase, too, in times where we couldn't get a handle on occurrences and any knowledge of where to begin to understand the driving focus on those situations. It was a shorthand way of consoling each other, knowing that we, too, didn't quite "get it." During our adult lives, we have both shared a sense of familiarity with our thought processes and personal dealings with unknown territory. This, too, was the backdrop for my reasoning of dealing with my ex-spouse's clan. Bonds are forged from years of companionship and thinking blueprints.

But, having written this, something was surely amiss in the social setting in which my ex and I attempted a bizarre waltz of matrimony. My brother and his fiancé sent me a birthday gift of a terrific book by Dean Koontz and a gift card. Arriving earlier than my daughter's time for recognizing my special day, I opened the gifts and was delighted. I called to share my heartfelt thanks and then bought myself a small steak, little cake, and the animals some treats.

Tonight, we celebrate! My brother and his lady, now his wife, are finding easier sailing in their new life together...my daughters are moving ahead with lives full of promise...and my grandsons make my heart sing with joy and purpose. The addition of my granddaughter to the mix gives me a zest I had not imagined possible.

The book sent as a gift is Dean Koontz, *Seize the Night*. It's the tale of a man who suffers the inability to withstand direct sunlight and lives in the shadows as a hermit.

When his town struggles with kidnapped children, this adversity of his becomes a valuable asset to him in his quest to save the victims.

So it is in my life, perhaps not as dramatic in first showing. This strange adventure into the Dark Side – much like the TV show – seems also to have instilled in me new strength and the ability to evaluate without relinquishing hard won life skills of keeping one's own counsel and removing those whose presence serves as a "vexation," as described in the Desiderata. In this Now, life is genuinely warm, even with all the challenges.

So, just what have I learned in all this?

> There is darkness...but just as surely, the contrast of
> remarkable goodness abounds...

Fear itself needs to be studied...it can hold a being hostage and remold life in inhospitable ways...For me, fear is sliding away. I used to find the idea of "feeling gratitude" difficult...but now, feeling blessed, I get it.

> Focusing on more upbeat thoughts and ideas does make a
> difference...maybe not overnight...

Sometimes it's absolutely necessary to cut people, groups, and ideas from your life to enable this upward thought path to grow....

MULLING....

"Don't rely on someone else for your happiness and self worth. Only you can be responsible for that...accept who you are – completely; the good and the bad – and make changes as you see fit – not because you think someone else wants you to be different." ~ Stacey Charter

What happened to me after the fall of my own beliefs? I began my journey as a fairly bright, upbeat, and somewhat funny journeyer into life. My background consisted of many treks into a variety of religions, even to include Scientology. In my first writing, *Romance Stew,* I sought to find romance with all the trimmings. Dating and online encounters proved an amazing discovery – of self. I thought I had found "Mr. Right." In a most unusual way, I did. I needed to know both the light and dark sides of this excursion and even of myself.

The resulting marriage and its drawing down the curtain on the last act of that particular play brought about *Life in the Aftermath of a Narcissist* which I have now revamped to become *Life in the Aftermath of a Psychopath.* Such personal angst...and a glimmer of the redemption where one finally sees that there IS goodness - no matter how dark the tunnel before light is detected. I had held on for such a long stretch. My feeling was that I had paid my dues with eleven hour days working with and for the invalid mother-in-law, being given only two three-minute breaks and lunch. Now, there was a sore spot. My spouse had worked me and I exploded in anger after nights filled with tears, telling him that I demanded at the very least, a lunch break. He would be kinder and I would soften...the cycle seemed to exist in endless loops.

Later, living as separated from my spouse, I suffered what

I consider a serious crisis of faith. Stumbling on the writings of a doctor whose work on pharmaceutical medications and their overuse intrigued me, I also discovered this gentleman's unorthodox tenets that were his conviction of truth. They involved "End Times" and the obliteration of the planet. This in a way became a turning point for me. I allowed it all. Granted, I had my own baggage and such a burning desire to make the marriage "fit."

I had to stop seeking answers from outside myself. These views would not be mine. I was having a difficult enough time trying to understand my last few years and how I could have allowed myself into such a strange land. It occurred to me that I may have skipped some educational processes when coming to this lifetime because I surely felt ill prepared for this length of participation with a narcissist.

With the bright and yet differently attuned doctor, I seemed to be pulling bizarre lessons into my existence. It's possible to understand the idea of co-dependence from therapists. When trying to be "nice," we can give too much ground. So, it was now time to rethink courtesy. I am no longer the same person today. This trudging through an alien domain has been enlightening but also, surreal and very painful. It's almost as though I were being forced to awaken from old ideas and tried and true methods. To be perfectly honest, I'm not altogether sure what these precipitates of knowledge acquired by instruction will mean to me in the days and months ahead.

I only know that there is no turning back in time. I am on my own route of development. However, the blogs I've found, texts that have opened to me, and people with whom I've linked have added dimensions that were not in my realm of thought on a daily basis.

Dr. Scott Barry Kaufman who writes for *Psychology Today* is a most unusual presence with his educational spectrum in the field of

psychology and his perceptions of intelligence, creativity, imagination, and personality. He is a cognitive scientist interested in the evolution of our culture. He and Dr. Darold Treffert, a psychiatrist who studies autism and many people who are "abled differently," possess such amazingly expansive compassion.

My four years with a narcissist who dropped me on the whims of his tide of life, gave me a different perspective of people. I felt much like one suffering from relationship Stockholm Syndrome. Saying that I,myself, was responsible for my choices became a criticism pointed at me. I already felt the fear of questioning my sanity and my ability to evaluate others. So many honestly meant well with their airy ideas of "just let it go." "Let him and the life about which you had dreamed leave you." The attraction has been, I am sure, the root for many therapists deciding the recipient of the narcissist's negativity to be co-dependence. A bit like James' Marcher, I felt there was goodness in my spouse if I could but reach him.

I was not the same as the woman who ran excitedly into my husband's arms...ready to take my place as a member of a lifetime union. I pictured myself growing old with my man. We had covered   so much territory...I didn't want to begin again.

And yet....that last Christmas together opened a new idea for me. If I am now so unhappy, why not be willing to find the wherewithal to start to build my finances and plan on going the way alone. Even knowing this was a good plan, I so hoped that life would surprise me...that our lives as a couple would turn around. It quite simply was not to be. I no longer could offer refuge for him. I also **KNEW** too much now. I had refused to give myself over to trust him completely and had refused to sell my tiny home. He was correct – I did not trust him. My small house was the last asset I possessed and I planned not to be homeless...and to one day pass something down to my children.

Released Illusions

" Every person, all evens of your life, are there because you have drawn them there. What you choose to do with them is up to you." ~Richard Bach

It was finally time to release all the lost illusions...the death of dreams of romance...the ideas of right and wrong and the strength of the bond between a man and woman in marriage. His mother was the dominant and focal point of his world. After all, she had done so much for her sons in their youth. Now, she needed care and nurturing....

I had fought his expenditures for his mom's extra desires...the money given to the sons to keep them afloat....the help in time, money, and physical plane presence to his first wife...I had issues to handle, too.

Looking back at that evening so long ago, in the beginning, where I was to meet his manager and coworkers, the work situation changed and the boss with his manager were unable to meet the small group of my spouse's co-workers as they toasted us at a local restaurant bar. He was unhappy at the change from being center stage. As all the folks were leaving, he turned to me and asked in his piqued expression, "you've got the bill, right?"   And he left me there.

Soon after our marriage, we met my daughters with the grandsons at a campground about an hour from both our locations. My youngest grandson hurt his ankle and we soon discovered he had broken it when

falling off the step to the camper. Rushing to an emergency room, he was given wonderful care and we took him with his mom to their apartment. Normally, I would have stayed the night with my loved ones, but my husband was silent and totally depressed. He mentioned thoughts of suicide and I was afraid to leave him alone at the campgrounds. He refused to communicate at all until the next morning where he said it brought back memories of his own son's accident and how he hadn't responded as he immediately should have. This was but a sign of all to come in the months and years ahead. Nothing existed outside a connection to him and his core family unit of his mom, dad, two brothers, sons, and first wife. Nothing. When I returned to my little house, I had no funds and went without food while he and his family ate steak.

I was confused and frightened....but I carried on...thinking this was the life I had chosen and all that was required was time for change. I was naive.

In spite of all the upsets and loss of hopeful expectation, the heartbroken sense of failure marked my days. What was I to do with all the unrelenting angst of this predicament? I cried while taking my bath at night. Looking back over time to the first months of our marriage, I recalled asking my spouse if he married me for more than the money. He was flying high in his job and with his role of the grand provider to his folks and extended family.

He invited his son's three children to spend part of the summer with us. They lived with his son's ex-wife and they kept a long-distance relationship. On the trip to pick them up out-of-state, he let me know that I would be footing the bill. And he would have to work during the vacation. However, he felt sure I could use "quality time." I was stunned. I knew nothing of these children and their mother, the ex-wife to his son, had made no contact with me personally in handing over her young charges into my and our care.

I didn't understand the way this family operated. The kids were wonderful. Even so, the gnawing sense that I was simply a tool to be used haunted my conscious hours. I seemed to have become an ATM cash system and personal care attendant. I approached him with dark circles under my eyes – time as his mother's handmaid, his former sister-in-law's incessant boy-toy answering machine messages to him, the adult bipolar son who needed financial help and a chauffeur, the private and loving phone conversations with his ex-wife, the nurse down the road who dropped by on occasion to ask if he could come to use her hot tub...but, I was also welcome, the statements that I had made promises and done things about which I had no memory, and his total lack of interest in sexual intimacy about which we had shared exuberance before the vows all took a toll on my sense of self and stability of my own beliefs. My question seemed always to be, "did you marry me for more than my funds and do you find anything about me that you like?"

How horribly sad and what a statement that makes about myself. Why didn't I leave? Below the surface reasons were that my house was now used by my daughter and I had "obligations" with his family members. But, the real reason was that I still felt somehow I should be able to turn it all around. I had come to believe him that somehow it was my fault.

Some of my family members urged me to leave, take my funds, and go home for awhile. BUT I felt as though this was my last chance for romance . We had crossed so many obstacles and we still moved forward. Surely there would be a moment where change could be grasped.

I never saw the final determination for divorce at his request coming.

I was a ridiculously expectant personage in my wish for better times. I was unaware that I had outlived my usefulness and was to be set free. Somehow I simply had ignored all the signs, all the "notices" from him, and the style of me-first in which his family existed. The thought that I had earned my place for the long haul had comforted me as in our conversations where we knew a better future was coming. He did not wish to be dissuaded. It was much easier to start without all the baggage of upheaval – new conditions, new relationship, new life...a fresh start, except for his invalid mom, from the ground up.

Refusing all communication with me after his reconnection with a love from the past, I found myself in deep grief. I was lost in a sea of sadness and alone – more than I had ever felt possible. What had happened to the concept of working toward a tomorrow? He contacted me for something in that tunnel of grief to tell me that "once the psychic connection was made, it would always be there." That was like a fat new worm on the hook in my mouth. It gave me just a whiff of hope that my dream might be realized. The answers would have to come from within me. There would be no closure and no goodbyes. Time to write once again. Maybe seeing it in black and white might allow me to evaluate my own choices of the past...and now.

This is my reason for writing the book. I wanted others to know how the ordeal "felt," not just the definitions of various forms of mental condition. I wish for others to understand that they are not alone and there are avenues for aid.

I found myself emotionally exhausted and without any funds for counseling with a therapist, and none to use for an attorney. Filing pro se in the divorce, with no transportation to permit my presence in the courtroom, I hoped that my submitted attachments for my response would be considered. I do not believe that they were.

My now ex-spouse stated that we had been separated a year

- when, in fact, he informed me of his decision for a divorce a few brief weeks after our lovely Easter gathering.

The judge felt that the marriage of three plus years was so short as to have no real financial bearing - nothing mentioned of the $65,000 that was gone. Forty-five thousand that I could show was in the paperwork I filed against him in bankruptcy court but all I received was less than two thousand.

There are times when "justice" will not be located. Learning to let go...and now, for me, to find a renewed sense of God's presence...is a new path. A good one.

Coming so far, I still struggle with the financial devastation, but the emotional upheaval has diminished. Once again, I am free to create along a different avenue of life.

It has been a long ride, but the fun house is now in the past and I am working toward picking up the pieces. The aftermath exists with physical health issues due to stress. "Seeing what is" becomes the first step toward action and new direction...as well as accountability.

Ideas and dreams as well as discovery of one's
realities are fragile...share wisely and learn to keep
your own counsel...

Cherish the moments when there is a sublime sense of comfort
and well being...and remember how these feel...

Be grateful for the best in this moment in time...it seems to
multiply....

Know that we are each doing the best we can with the information available to us and our own state of ability...

We are individuals, but we are also part of greater societies...

We learn in spurts and this grand experimentation is simply and cleanly a tentative procedure of supposition...

We each don't have to be *right*...we must each be as ethical as we are capable of understanding values and motives relating to human conduct...and this will change as we develop...

We need to reach out for help and contact to avoid being stuck in any emotional position along this journey...

"I am my heart's undertaker. Daily I go and retrieve its tattered remains, place them delicately into its little coffin, and bury it in the depths of my memory, only to have to do it all again, tomorrow."

~ Emilie Autumn

19

Passion's Melancholy Memory

What I DID miss was the possibility of passion. Knowing that another man in my life was not the "magic bullet," I began to find interest in other activities. In all honesty, this was a very slow procedure. Daily activities came and went. Time crawled by. One day I found that I simply hadn't thought about him, his family, the heartache, and the loss. And writing fell into its cathartic role. I was me, and there it lay out in the open...I had been left behind.

The Right to Fall Down

Perhaps the greatest quest of this lifetime exists to be true to ourselves. Joining another in marriage should not precipitate giving away oneself and yet, compromise and respect for the values of the entity of the union must mesh with those of both individuals.

This state of having something in common with shared efforts and

interests should entail a mutual "glue" and loyalty. The couple's association is to bolster both individuals as well as the life force of the marriage. Betrayal in one form or another is always a shock for one of the party's to discover. It might even be a surprise to the one committing offense that the bond was not so strong that such a change in choice might occur.

Dr. Roberta Temes and Geoffrey Gorer discuss three stages of grief for people left behind. Their model finds a base with the loss in the death of another, but it seems most applicable to the displaced spouse, as well. They posit that grief is not a disease and there is no magic pill for a cure, but it does have an end. "Numbness, disorganization and reorganization are these stages and they bring about emotional, physical and behavioral changes in all of us."

The works of Temes and Gorer list numbness as the first stage - a place for the automatic pilot which also includes genuine sorrow, moments of anger, and even guilt. In disorganization, the next phase, a constant and acute loneliness accompanies the loss along with physical symptoms such as tightness in the throat, shortness of breath, and anxiety with panic. This second phase may be wrenching and we are advised to feel all the emotions and not keep them bottled. Eventually, the promise is that (1) we will complete the emotional process and (2) we will begin to focus our energy toward a future.

In the final stage of reorganization, the sadness and weeping subside and the one left behind begins to trust again in himself to provide a   security on his own.

Although the authors intended to assist in the experience of the death of a loved one, this message and sense of hope proves valuable to the spouse who found him/herself to be so easily discarded. The advice for obtaining a support system should be underscored.

Looking at life from the perspective of the disposable spouse, the self-esteem and trust in ability to fill certain roles finds a difficult path. Intimacies and openness of thoughts, joys, and upsets may have been turned inward trying to comprehend what actually transpired in the decision of the other partner to end the union. As one who was so quickly left behind, I found myself suffering anxiety over thoughts of "what if" and "were there unspoken boundaries and topics upon which I was not to communicate."

Betrayal is as personal as we are as individuals. Mine included a primary loyalty to parents, an ex-wife with her extended family, and the depletion of my funds brought into the marriage. Marriage counseling seemed a one-time interest for the departing spouse. My sadness and deep hurts came from the rites of passage over infatuations with other women, a lack of interest in me as a woman, and the absence of meaningful communication. Having felt that I had "paid my dues" and was allowed to voice opposing ideas, I erred for the facade my spouse needed to perpetuate as well as his need to play the single entity.

In my own capturing of knowledge and practical wisdom, I can see that I was so enthralled by the vision of what life would be as the future moved

into focus that I failed to fully evaluate the discrepancies of acceptability in the joint venture.

Ideas of honor and commitment must be shared. Expecting maturity in responsibilities may not be accessible if the partner finds that his role no longer serves the purpose for which it was created. Life often brings cycles and should one be unprepared for the bumps along the path, that proverbial "grass is greener" elsewhere mentality may be ever so enticing.

Is hope just beyond the next night-fall? Yes, but there is work on self and handling grief to be accomplished first. We will find that we don't look toward that departed spouse for aid or compassion...or answers and when that day arrives, it will be comforting that we can be fine just as a lone person. There will come a time when thoughts will not automatically drift toward the deceased union and the "what if's" of one's choices in behavior and response.

We have a right to fumble, err, and fall down. We also have the right to see that our best efforts could not manifest the joint vision without both giving to that manifestation. Helen Rowland summarizes the subject well in "A Guide" to Men": "When two people decide to get a divorce, it isn't a sign that they "don't understand" one another, but a sign that they have, at last, begun to."

God speed. Writing this while attempting to understand my place in

the universe, I saw that the dream was only that and I simply didn't have enough common ground or agreement to make it take shape in the here and now. The man who had been my husband and the family I had thought appreciated me were only apparitions in a mist of my own making. They never took off their masks.

Full Circle, and yet...

"We shall not cease from exploration
And the end of all our exploring Will
be to arrive where we started
And know the place for the first time." ~T.S. Eliot

So, poorer in the sense of financial existence, and carrying increased compassion along with the hope of improved emotional well being, I began this leg of the journey. I am genuinely pleased that I no longer fantasize about my ex-spouse being hit by an 18-wheeler. My humor is returning and life is so much more than Joseph Conrad's dark writings. In his novella, The Heart of Darkness, he explores the study of civilized man versus the native man. I will say that I find the idea of a fallible narrator to fit my ideas of this lifetime presently.

My time within the clan of my ex-spouse proved costly on many levels, but also taught me about the sense of loyalty in belonging. It takes courage to "let go" and honor to acknowledge one's own part in the drama that unfolded. I've come full circle from writing my book, *Romance Stew*.

Once again with courage in hand.....I look newly at my passion for life....and fondly remember the gal I was...

Risk is everywhere, and so is adventure. One can voice hopes and dreams. The "stakes might be high" and we don't want to disappoint or be disappointed. We can also choose to be as romantic as we wish and be free with compassion, kindness, tenderness, and even hint at forthcoming passion, knowing the recipient doesn't need to be Mr. of Ms. Right.

Sometimes you just jump, and learn to fly on the way down.

My approach to life will rejuvenate itself....

From TheHitchhikers'GuidetotheGalaxy:

"The Book: Curiously the only thing that went through the mind of the bowl of petunias, as it fell, was, 'Oh no, not again.' Many people have speculated that if we knew exactly *why* the bowl of petunias had thought that we would know a lot more about the nature of the universe than we do now. "

Resiliency, and thus it flows.....

After-thoughts

From Craig Huston of successstransformation.com, I received a fascinating video called, "Paper Airplane." It's a thought-provoking story about vision, courage and a sixth grader's unique response to a class project.

In class, a sixth grade teacher has created an assignment of working with a partner on paper aircraft to determine which style of design would travel the farthest.

The class studied aerodynamics all week and then the day of the race arrived.

The planes looked similar, but some

did better and some not as well.

Near the end, the one team had a partner who had not made a shaped craft by folding the paper. His

friend's flew pretty well....if the partner could only make his paper into one flying a similar length of distance, the pair could win the race.

The partner brought his unfolded paper to the line for launch...AND scrunched it INTO a BALL.

It sailed farther than anyone's plane.

One step at a time...

The future is a canvas open to delightful possibilities....

"What a weird <efing> drug. And we're just coming out of it and we're kind of waking up." ~ **Robin Williams**

20
Decide Which Shore

There exists so much joy and astonishing broadening of my own personal life thread now. **I can say that I am seeing miracles in the sphere of the smallest of daily activities.**

This is the culmination.   As Morgan Freeman's character as God in "Bruce Almighty " would say, "it's good."

Spirit really is the three dimensional world.   As I re-establish myself in this magnificent realm of creativity and choice, I find the most amazing authors of truly great self-help works. Not quick fixes but thinking men. Og Mandino has become a favorite. His book, *The Choice,* offers a warm invitation to believe that we are each one-of-a-kind and remarkable.   There is a reason we are here in this moment.

I am now turning the page on the past and looking with wonder at the next tomorrow, while living today as fully as possible.   The surge of enthusiasm encourages me – and everyone – to have gratitude, trust that each of us can leave others better for our contact, and the excitement that something grand is unfolding. The choice is to begin in this very moment. We each have gifts to unwrap and share.

There exists great joy in knowing we are not alone and that uplifting paths are right before us. The withdrawing into a kernel of self most probably befell all of us who experienced time with a psychopath. As I know more about people this day, I will work to treat others I meet with care, kindness, and understanding. As Mandino says, "your life will never be the same again." Perhaps this is TRUST in God and HIS Universe...My universe.

Helplessness is the ruse.

When this particular life school lesson developed, I felt terrifically vulnerable and overcome. The perceptions bring real sensations of chaos and unprotectedness but they are not certifiably genuine as far as the essence of who each of us is. We can fall into situations and feelings with the best of intentions. Being vigilant about the thoughts and wishes that we use to steer our lives persists as mandatory. Life should be full of joyful endeavor. We must stand up to the myriad conflicting precepts that lie in our subconscious such as duty and honor as we seek to honestly exact the reality of scenes, situations, and relationships. It is OK to acknowledge that we desire an exchange for our input into creating a dream.

It offers camaraderie to obtain the agreement of others, but at the end of the day, each of us works the magic of this life in making our very own and quite special styles of presence. I am writing this last of my brief series to show others that there is not only light at the end of the tunnel, but that the conduit of passage is part of who we are.

In Ursula Le Guin's *The Lathe of Heaven,* the villainous and power-seeking therapist exists ONLY as a character in our protagonist's mind as our hero actually is the author of the universe that he has concocted. The movie version has the psychologist running insanely down a tunnel toward the-end-of-the-world's firestorm when he comes to realize that he is only a player. Just maybe that is how we acted in this strange encounter with *what is.* The time has arrived for us to look within to perceive our own power and discern ***what is.***

By detaching from observing yourself as Vernon Howard would say, we can all look at the fallout from particular paths chosen.

There is never a point of no return to re-evaluate and change direction. Emmet Fox writes:"It is not possible that you could ever find yourself anywhere where God was not fully present, fully active, able and willing to set you free."   Free will is a bugger only in the sense that we might not allow ourselves to see this. We cannot control others, but we have the gift of stupendous power to regulate   and   switch   our   thoughts   and   behaviors. If we are each honest, we might rail against not getting our way

in the creating process. Because we all have this force of authorship, each is making his own book and we work together. However, not all share the same goals, emotional values, and virtues, not to mention methodologies. It is OK to let go of that particular connection. For
me, it felt as if I were so deeply alone. I now understand and conclude that was never the case. Being trapped for me left me bereft of alternate viewpoints.   It remains easy to say, "take another path." I suspect this is the reason we go to books. On our own we can't quite muster the willpower and strength to believe there is life-beyond-this-upsetting-moment.

It's here. It's waiting. Be kind to yourself as it may require baby steps. It will require grabbing an idea of positive action and idea and removing yourself from negativity. The fear of loss may raise its flaming face, but each of us can replace that something unbearable with a new breath of "maybe." We must release the old dream and look for a new one. But first, we must each look within ourselves and seek to understand choices. There exists always some exchange from those – feeling better, fulfilled, not alone. That's the tough part. When the scales have tipped from joy to unhappiness, now it must require the light of truth of our reality. Let go.

Vernon Howard shares a great story about a man losing his hat in the wind and it flies into a part of the forest where men have not been. The wild animals gather around trying to decide what the hat is and what could be the use. An owl reports that he has seen men who wear hats on their heads. The animals who have no knowledge of this creature called man dismiss the owl and continue their discussions. This is the way we all act when faced with an obstacle. Sometimes we must each reach outside our comfort zones. They may not be so *comfortable* after all.

"Normal is nothing more than a cycle on a washing machine." ~
Whoopi Goldberg

TWEAKING A BIT

Thank you for reading my ideas. I genuinely hope that seeing the imperfections in me will give you a lift in your own thoughts of "what if."

No one needs to *settle.* I watched some amazing Ted Talks about altruism. A fascinating subject. Animals seem to exhibit behaviors described as altruistic and cooperative from a larger picture, too. We humans are indeed a most complex mix of demonstrations. Having money and a sense of protection from the standpoint of being outside of abject poverty may result in a more fluid altruistic approach. However, when push comes to shove, that unselfish regard for the well being of others often shines forth in the majority of us humans.

Here is a thought of my own. Today, I could indeed be altruistic, much more than in my pre-psychopath era. I feel that, like *Alice Through the Looking Glass*, I have experienced a land that I found hard to comprehend and have witnessed my attitude and actions within that arena. Altruistic acts go beyond empathy and compassion. These require ACTION to make a difference. And action is accompanied by strength to venture onward.

Courage stands as a most interesting phenomenon. It isn't feeling fearless, it forges ahead in spite of any agonizing worry. This deed demands acknowledging one's moral compass. Each of us simply must set our own ground rules for behavior and stick with these. Because a sense that we might lose something if we don't acquiesce may urge us to keep to ourselves, we at times close our thoughts.

Although not one who really *meditates* in any traditional sense, I have begun to think of something positive at least once a day and to do so for more than just a few moments. I find that I am quite surprised and elated to note that I feel immense gratitude suddenly. Coupling this, I enjoy spending time outside my four walls – a walk, working on the house or yard, or just the enjoyment of nature.

Do all my concerns – a car malfunctioning, need for more income, or upsets regarding others – mysteriously vanish? Perhaps not, but somehow bit by bit, my life improves. For me, this is part of my returning trust in God. It is part of a growing and quiet confidence that I have a purpose in this old plane of existence. There really is no such thing as defeat (thought of Vernon Howard). The dreams within goals that I have previously postulated held deadlines (taken from Napoleon Hill) and those time frames may not jive with the flow of energy in this moment's sphere of reality. So, I can begin a discussion with myself of sorts. Small adjustments might be necessary. *"We must reinvent a future free of blinders so that we can choose from real options."* ~David Suzuki, academic and activist

Humor has helped me tremendously.
Maybe there is something to learn from a strange and oddball experience or situation. I like George Carlin's idea: "*Some people see the glass as half full. Others see it half empty. I see a glass that's twice as big as it needs to be.*"

As I close this last chapter, I send you gentle energy, kindness and a deep and caring faith in YOU that you will find your own path...this is your story AND you are NOT ALONE! Keep that passion and look up....look outward....feel this moment....and breathe.

As Robin Williams said, "We don't read and write poetry because it's cute. We read and write poetry because we are members of the human race. And the human race is filled with passion. And medicine, law, business, engineering – these are noble pursuits and necessary to sustain life. But poetry, beauty, romance, love – these are what we stay alive for."

ABOUT THE AUTHOR

Becky Reed lives in Montana in a lovely cottage-home in town. Her daughters with their husbands and her three amazing grandchildren live across town. Living in the old section called Goosetown, she has done a great deal of work on her tiny home. She is a seeker and a believer in the goodness that abounds...no matter the struggles and hurdles.

From a Jewish Magazine:
A man seeks his Rabbi's advice because he thinks his wife is trying to poison him.

The Rabbi decides to visit the wife to check the situation.

Returning to the husband, he calmly says,
"Take the Poison."

Once upon a time a woman awoke. The upsetting dream departed. Yes, she remembered it, but she also knew as she gazed at her adult children with their spouses, grandchildren, her home, and her pets that some grand essence overflows with joyous hopefulness. Einstein puts it well: "When you are courting a nice girl, an hour seems like a second. When you sit on a red-hot cinder a second seems like an hour."